Lesson of Love

Prue Phillipson

© 2000 Trustees for Methodist Church Purposes

Front Cover Photo: © Digital Vision

ISBN   1 85852 153 X

Introduction

One in every five people over 80 live with dementia. In an ageing society it is very important that we all understand more about Alzheimer's disease and similar conditions. Such books as *Lesson of Love* will help us to do this.

This enlightening true-life story captures the love of the carer for her mother and the love of God as they journey together into uncharted waters. The author manages to achieve a 'person-centred approach', offering endless care and supervision as her mother becomes increasingly physically and mentally frail.

The story combines humour, tragedy and endless testings of their relationship and constant turning to God in prayer. This brings Prue's mother contentment, satisfaction and a presence in the final months of her life.

More and more work is being undertaken to capture the religious and spiritual feelings of older people living with diseases such as Alzheimer's. At Methodist Homes we are pleased to say that, through the commitment and ongoing interest of our care staff, chaplains and volunteers, we continue to witness to God's love in this way.

Many older people turn to prayer at the end of their lives. As they prepare to meet their Maker, we must never presume that those living with dementia ever lose their faith, rather that many will find themselves nearer to God as the living world becomes an increasingly difficult place in which to communicate.

Michael Broughton
Dementia Services Adviser
Methodist Homes for the Aged

Why this book?

Nine years after my mother's death I am able to reread the journal I kept during the last four years of her life and to realise that my experience might help others to cope better than I did. Certainly I wouldn't have coped at all without faith in Jesus Christ. However dark the valley his presence was there. But this isn't a dark book. The steps on the journey were occasionally comical though often painful, but the uplifting moments were full of an intensity of joy which was not of this world. I was led into a deeper understanding of what it really means to follow Christ and not only was I blessed but the rest of the family was too, as well as our friends and the many carers who helped us. But I have regrets that I could have done better and this is why I feel bound in thankfulness for God's blessings to write this little book.

Mother – a biographical sketch

My mother was born in November 1899, the sixth of eight children in a talented, artistic and devoutly Christian family. In days of low pay and strict regime she trained as a nurse but had to leave work when she married my father, a solicitor, though she returned to help out at a local hospital during the Second World War. They had two girls of whom I was the younger.

We lived in Newcastle upon Tyne and Mother in fact occupied the same house from 1935 to 1981 when she came to live near me and my family in Hexham. This was twenty years after my father's sudden death from a heart attack and two years after my sister's death from a brain tumour. Mother grittily stuck it alone for nearly two years, close to her church and friends. We saw her often and she came on holidays with us but she was very strong and independent and wanted to stay in her own home.

However, when she had a severe bout of sciatica she had to come and stay with us and by the time she was better the beauty of the small market town of Hexham and its surrounding country, the friendliness of my neighbours and the congregation at the Abbey where we worshipped convinced her she would be happy here. In God's providence a bungalow fifty yards down the lane dividing our house from our back garden came up for sale. It had a garden which she loved, beautiful trees and a south-facing patio with distant views. She said she had come to heaven.

Although she was eighty-two when she moved in she worked at her two main hobbies of gardening and painting. She was a considerable water-colourist and we joined the local Art Club where she made many friends. In fact wherever she went she made friends; she was interested in people, eager to help, always putting others before herself.

We had had five children and at this time our two boys were still at school, Mark in his last year, Gavin thirteen. Our eldest daughter, Helen, a teacher, was married and had her first child; the next, Claire, was married and a social worker, and Katherine was at university. So we were a large family with plenty of comings and goings but Mother loved it all and entered into family occasions with joy and enthusiasm and her usual helpfulness. Her health was good and she walked at a pace and worked with the energy of someone in their sixties rather than their eighties. This was the situation up to the beginning of the change.

1
The Beginning of the Change

It was a July day in 1984, the garden wet from a morning shower but heavy with summer and ripening fruit. I ran along the lane to tell Mother I was going to pick raspberries so she wouldn't wander into the house looking for me. In two minutes she arrived in a plastic mac with a bowl.

'I've come to help,' she said.

We hadn't been picking long before the sun came out and the raspberry canes steamed in the warm air. And it wasn't just the canes that were warming up. I hadn't thought anything about Mother still wearing her plastic mac and working away, reaching and stooping by turns. Then all at once I heard her from the other side of the canes mumble something in a strange voice and the next moment she had collapsed on the ground.

Much alarmed I slid a garden cushion under her head and ran for a neighbour with nursing training. She helped revive Mother and together we managed to get her into the house and on to the settee. She was trying to tell us she was quite all right but her speech was blurred and I feared the worst. I sent a wordless 'arrow' prayer for God's help and healing.

In ten minutes the doctor was there and confirmed that she had had a slight stroke. However, by evening she had perked up and her speech was almost normal again. I put her to bed in 'her' room, the one she had had for six months while the bungalow sale went through and in a few days she was demanding to go back to her bungalow and seemed perfectly well again. She and all of us gave thanks to God.

The only effect we noticed was a slight memory loss, particularly of people's names, but physically she was bounding with energy again and walking as fast as ever. A Newcastle minister used to tease her that she was 'the fastest woman' he knew. She loved that!

Prue and Mother (aged 83, still game for anything)

It was the following March when she again succumbed to hot steamy conditions, this time at the hairdresser's. I was telephoned to say she had suffered a cardiac arrest and had been taken to hospital. I drove there all of a tremble and sat outside the intensive care unit, praying that I would be able to speak to her and say goodbye. My mind was obsessed with the memory that we had parted rather brusquely that morning because she had insisted on walking to the hairdresser's when I wanted to give her a lift. She had gone off in a hurry and I was now afraid that she might have strained her heart before she even arrived. I kept telling God that she couldn't die on me till I had been able to give her a loving kiss and see that warm smile of hers in response.

I sat for quarter of an hour and then the door opened and out she came on a trolley, wrapped in silver foil and joking with the porter. Speechless with astonishment I followed behind as she was wheeled to the ward. Then I sat with her and gently explained what had happened. She was quite unconcerned about herself, only sorry that I had had such a fright and that she must have caused a lot of bother at the hairdresser's. When it was lunchtime she sat up and ate a good meal! I kept thanking God. I just couldn't believe that she seemed completely herself again.

But she wasn't completely herself. During the few days she stayed under observation in hospital I began to notice little signs of confusion. I brought her several books because she always loved reading and one of them posed a real problem for her because the back cover had a blurb about another book by the same author. After she had read a few chapters she commented, tapping the blurb, 'It doesn't seem to be turning out like this.'

I laughed. 'It wouldn't be. It's not the same book.' I said it lightly and casually and she seemed to be smiling and nodding. She had always been extremely quick on the uptake. But on the next visit and the next and the next she pointed to the cover again and said with genuine bewilderment, 'I'm still waiting to find out when all this happens.' I was really shocked to realise that, though in all other respects her mind was as alert and clear as ever, she could neither grasp nor retain my explanation.

I wish now that a nurse or doctor had told me she might have the odd 'blind spot'. It's so easy to show irritation if you're asked the same thing over and over again by someone apparently normal who thinks *you* are making a poor fist of clarifying the matter. Anyway we let the book rest as somehow inexplicable and Mother came home, grew fit again in the springtime and by May was given the all-clear by the doctor to go on holiday with us.

The first thing we noticed was that she had trouble finding her bedroom in the cottage. She would go to the bathroom and then reappear in the living room in her dressing-gown, laughing at herself.

'I know it's ridiculous,' she would say, 'but which is my room?'

We saw the same confusion of her spatial sense appear in her paintings. A headland would lie above the sea's horizon or trees would be growing in the waves. The sad thing was that she knew something was wrong but couldn't correct it. She still had a lovely touch with her brush and her sense of colour was as good as ever. It was the arrangement of things on a page that seemed to have deserted her. I was embarrassed because she loved me to paint with her and always praised what I was doing though I was never the painter she had been. But it was her nature to remain bright and cheerful and I couldn't even now say how much it was troubling her.

After we came home and were in familiar surroundings again we fell back into our usual ways of going shopping together and often parting to do separate errands before meeting up again. This was the cause of much exasperation for both of us.

'If you'd *said* you were going to wait at the Post Office –'

'But I did, Mother, several times. You repeated it –'

It seems so obvious, looking back, that her short-term memory was quite swiftly ebbing away. But at the time it just didn't square with the fact that she was still her independent, active self, running her own home, having visitors to tea or coffee, beavering away in her garden.

We argued too over her working too hard at gardening. Mark and Gavin cut her lawns but she still loved to get down on a kneeler to weed and on summer evenings I would sometimes find her still out at nine o'clock. I had a big garden of my own to see to and I felt that the standard of tidiness she expected in her own was beyond a joke, but then she had always been a perfectionist. Eventually we got her a gardener to come once a week. For the heavier work in the house I had a wonderful help of long years who came one week to Mother's bungalow and the next to me. When she was there she and Mother lunched together and I had time off for my writing.

But by early autumn this kind helper and I had seen new problems. One day Mother put her electric kettle on the gas stove but luckily I discovered it before serious damage was done. We decided it would be safer to leave her with only the hob kettle. Later she was to burn out four of these before I hid her matches and took over all her household activities.

But that point had not been reached when Gavin resumed school in September and Mother and I were on our own again all day. We ate lunch together in her bungalow or on her patio if it was warm enough, and usually I made it with her bustling about helping. But I knew she liked to feel she was the hostess so I wasn't surprised when one morning she came trotting along the lane after breakfast saying she had prepared the vegetables and what would I like with them? I said we could have omelettes which I'd make when I came over at twelve. She was back at eleven saying, 'How should we have the eggs cooked?' I repeated that we'd have omelettes in an hour's time, but she came back about quarter to twelve saying lunch was ready.

I got up from my typewriter and followed her. I had been hard at work and I thought how lucky I was to have Mother, who had cooked wonderful meals for us all since our childhood, and was still able to prepare something tasty for me in her eighties.

When I saw what it was I didn't know whether to laugh or cry. In the pressure cooker two eggs, still in their shells, were floating among bits of potato and cabbage with grated cheese melted in the water too.

'Is this all right?' she said. 'I wasn't sure how you wanted the eggs done.'

She looked anxious and I'm glad that I said, 'It's fine.'

We strained off the water and broke the slightly coddled eggs over the vegetables, added some more cheese and both pretended it was a lovely meal.

It was this incident that triggered my decision to keep a diary. I needed to detach myself from what was happening so that I wouldn't react all the time. I could laugh it off – one more for the diary! I still had no idea where all this was heading. I only knew that even when I was doing the cooking I could be very irritated by her standing over me watching as if everything was new and strange.

'Oh well, we all have our own ways of doing things,' she would say as I basted a chicken exactly as she had always taught me.

'You were doing it like this before I was born,' I couldn't help saying.

She would just shake her head, smiling. 'It's all right. I like to see what you do.'

I'm not the sort of person who starts tearing their hair out but I had to learn to cope with this without getting into arguments. I don't think at this stage that I was praying about Mother's condition at all or even realising that she *had* a condition and that I was going to need God's help with it. After all, she was still able to go about and hold perfectly normal conversations with people and they would never suspect a thing. No one but the immediate family knew there was anything wrong at all.

If I am honest I must admit that my prayers were mostly for the younger generation, their marriages, careers, and how they would bring up their families. I prayed that the strong faith which my parents had imparted to me would flow on to them. Mother was the old, secure generation and, in physical health, was wonderful for her age. It's strange that I had up to this point been blind to the one area of my life where prayer would make all the difference to my attitude. For though specific prayers are sometimes answered in a very plain way I am sure that the biggest change as a result of prayer is in ourselves. And yet I neglected to pray about what was then my greatest cause of daily exasperation!

Still, for my own sanity and to try to see the funny side of things, I began, on 14th November 1985 'The Diary of Mother'.

2

Beginning the Journal with Prayer

I began the diary with the words 'I must keep in mind that these oddities of behaviour in my mother are not her conscious and deliberate acts.'

It seems extraordinary now that it had taken me till then to spell this out clearly in my mind. I can only reiterate that Mother was her old self for ninety per cent of the time and still full of vigour. I know now that this is often the case with the onset of senile dementia and that the physical energy just makes the mental lapses harder to cope with. But it is so important that the carer understands this and I wish now I had been better prepared for what was to come.

However, beginning the journal did make me aware at last of the need to pray for help. It was all very well to laugh when I realised why, for example, she said her tea tasted odd. I found she was putting a teabag in a cup and adding the milk before the boiling water. But what was distressing was that she could get quite upset if I pointed out her mistakes. Once I found her putting her stainless steel teapot on the gas to stew the tea. I had to think of all sorts of ways of stopping disasters without appearing to correct her, which was very wearing. So, for my own sake, I did begin to ask for God's help.

I think I have never been very good at what some people call their prayer time. People who talk about a half-hour prayer time, morning and evening, quite unintentionally leave me feeling ashamed. It's true we've always held family prayers at the beginning and ending of each day as my parents did – a Bible reading, a short prayer, the Lord's Prayer and the blessing, but my own private prayers are more haphazard. When governed by an immediate need they are most earnest but I have always found it difficult to focus my mind for very long when my body is idle. So my best times for communing with God are when my hands are busy – with housework or gardening.

Sometimes when I'm weeding rows of lettuces I allot a row to a particular friend or family member and bear that person before the Lord till I come to the next row. I feel sure the Lord accepts many different ways of coming to him and as he has granted me abundant health and energy I trust he understands how hard I find it to sit or kneel for long periods of physical immobility and keep my mind concentrated. I know I should be listening to him or meditating on a sentence from Scripture, not necessarily asking for anything at all, just resting in his love, but too often my imagination flies about out of control.

I remember, however, that I did kneel on my bed that day I began 'The Diary of Mother' and I prayed for the gift of patience. At once the simple answer came into my heart: LOVE. No other word, just LOVE. When I waited quietly, trying to open my heart to anything else God would reveal, there was still only LOVE. I didn't even at that moment feel the warmth of *his* love. I just had that one word, LOVE.

I lay down and thought about it. I could see that I had a lesson to learn about love and I didn't pray any more but reflected on what this meant.

First of all I realised that it wasn't enough to hold back a very human impatience. What I had been doing so often was biting back annoyance because I knew I would feel uncomfortably guilty afterwards if I put it into words. That was 'goodness' governed by self, the sort of righteousness which is described in the Bible as 'filthy rags'. Far from being love it was totally egotistical. Love was positive, not negative. In human terms it might be laudable to manage a whole day without being cross. But God wasn't praising that. God was expecting more, much more. Was I up to it? Could I rise to such expectations?

I knew he wouldn't leave me without help. I knew that he loved me. I knew that he loved Mother. And did I not love him, first, before Alan, Mother and all the family? That was what I had to focus on, to let my heart dwell on his loving heart. Then, if the love in my heart was pure, arising out of my love for him, I wouldn't have to restrain my tongue because I would feel no irritation. Mother too would sense my love and not resent my interference.

Well, I knew this and believed it and resolved that it would always light my way. But I can see clearly now that I was only at the beginning of a long learning experience. And yet I had been a Christian all my life, calling on my faith to see me through many periods of trial. Mostly it was the sense of eternity which had enabled me to keep things in perspective. Even as a child I can remember finding relief from the worries which can grip the young out of all proportion to their significance, by saying to myself, 'This won't matter in God's kingdom.' I often prayed too to 'the God of Abraham,

Isaac and Jacob' and was reassured by a sense of his immensity.

As children my sister and I were given wonderful resources for our spiritual life – a knowledge of the Bible, regular worship, the catechism lovingly explained, as well as the solid background of a happy family extending on both sides to uncles, aunts and cousins who shared the same faith in the same Lord. What amazing riches! But to explore them, to use them daily and to draw closer to the One at the heart of them involves a lifetime of experience, and all the time the Christian is struggling against the world's attitudes, which, increasingly, are totally contrary.

In the world's eyes humble acceptance of limitations in one's daily sphere has almost become a sin. Everything that restricts one's life is called 'a problem' and a problem has to have a solution which the government or some other body should provide if one can't find it for oneself. People are urged to assert themselves, to claim their rights, to seek self-fulfilment at all costs. Elements of this attitude, which in terms of man's history is quite recent, have permeated both educational theory and the ideal of the welfare state. The fruits appear beneficial when the attitude is one of love and compassion for others, but its roots are not in the God who gave himself for us in total sacrifice. The very word 'sacrifice' has become suspect. Well-meaning people frequently say, reproachfully, 'Now you mustn't sacrifice yourself' or 'You can't sacrifice your life for someone else, it's not right.' Jesus never said this. In fact he said that laying down one's life for another was the highest test of love. At the same time he is the ultimate judge and those who cruelly and selfishly exploit others will come face to face with him and be called to account.

I was in my late fifties when Mother began to deteriorate mentally, yet I still had to make constant fresh resolutions to practise in thought, word and deed, from a heart of love, what I knew well enough in my head. In fact I know now that I rarely drew fully on God's boundless love, the true source of strength, to carry out my resolutions, which was why I often failed. And I was also, as time went on, frequently led into the world's viewpoint of Mother as 'a problem'. Rereading my diary has shown me how very easy it was to slip into this way of thinking. But I had been given the word and I knew where to seek that love which, like his peace, passes all understanding.

3
Independence and Illness

At this stage of Mother's condition the most time-consuming and frustrating of my tasks was hunting for things. The journal recalls daily searches for letters, bills, her purse, her handbag, her pension book. Mother was always tidy and would pop things away in case anyone called. One entry on market day was typical:

> Today I *couldn't* find her handbag and had to lend her money for shopping. Now she'll be convinced for the rest of the week that she owes me something. She doesn't because I looked tonight under her folded best dressing-gown on the top shelf of her wardrobe and there was her bag. I let her take the money out herself and pay me back, but I've no hope she'll remember.

It was the waste of time that exasperated me and I gave more thought to how I could avoid this than I did to remembering my lesson of love. On the next market day I saw her bag lying in the kitchen so I took it and her shopping trolley to my house after breakfast, telling her over and over again that I had it and that all she had to do was put her coat on and come to me when she was ready. She repeated several times, 'Darling, I know you've got it. I'm not a fool.' But she didn't come, so I went over and found she had turned the bungalow upside down looking for her bag. When I reminded her I'd taken it she said, 'Well, I didn't know, did I?'

An allied difficulty was how to avoid making her feel incapable. On 3rd December I wrote one brief, poignant entry. 'Today Mother said, "I feel about six when I go out with you."' I know I was hurt but I couldn't see where I'd gone wrong. The answer was more pure, more perfect love which would have meant that she couldn't feel belittled by anything I said or did.

At this stage she could still read the clock and expected to make and keep arrangements. I usually made her an early appointment at the hairdresser's once a fortnight and Alan ran her there on his way to work. She knew she had to come over to our house about 8.45 which was no problem as she was an early riser.

On 4th December I wrote:

> I looked out of the back door and saw her
> trotting along the lane at 8.48. Great – till I
> noticed she had two dresses on! Should I say
> anything? No, she'd hate to keep Alan waiting
> and would be terribly embarrassed if he knew
> what she'd done. I think when she got in the
> car that she saw one hem below the other. She
> looked slightly puzzled. I said with a big smile,
> 'That's all right,' and off they went. It wasn't
> till bedtime that she fully realised. I just
> laughed and said, 'Well, it kept you warm.' I
> find a light-hearted approach works well
> sometimes. She's still got a sense of humour.
> She asked me after tea if I had a meeting
> tonight and when I said, 'No, I've got nothing
> on,' she said, quick as a flash. 'Mind you don't
> get cold then!' I love it when she's like this.

In St Paul's 'fruit of the Spirit' love is placed first, then joy. I quickly discovered how much they go hand in hand. When I felt happy Mother responded readily; we had many laughs together and my human love overflowed to her and hers to me. What I had to learn was a divine love and joy which could keep on flowing whatever the response, and that could only happen through the activity of the Holy Spirit.

Mother was still her own happy self for most of the time and loved to see all the family. We had a beautiful Christmas that year. Gavin was now singing in the men's choir at the Abbey and had the solo in 'The Three Kings'. We were all there at the carol service on Christmas Eve and on Christmas Day. Helen's family came for lunch and to stay over till Boxing Day. Mother loved her little great-granddaughter, Clare, now five. She was always wonderful with children and had seen us through all sorts of crises when our five were still young and we lived not far from her in Newcastle.

I made no entries in the journal over Christmas and New Year. I suppose I was just too busy with a full house but I know that Mother had us all to tea on Christmas Day and though I had made most of the preparations she felt she was keeping up the old tradition of a candlelit tea at her house and this made her very happy. She beamed round on everyone, the loving, generous hostess, plying her guests with goodies till they could eat no more.

And then, sadly, she caught a bad cold in early January which led to a chest infection and quite suddenly I found myself a full-time nurse. On 15th February 1986 I summed up what had been happening since the last diary entry: 'It's a long time since I've written anything. There's been no improvement. In fact, as Mother has had a cold which turned into bronchitis, she deteriorated for a while.' Seeing these words now I realise I was still half-expecting Mother's mental state to be fully restored.

The diary continues:

> When she was ill she was very sleepy and
> needed encouragement to eat and drink. She
> weighed only just over seven stones at her
> worst. Of course, I've been putting her to bed
> each night and helping her to dress in the
> morning on the days when she was well
> enough to get up. But as she's got stronger
> she's become more assertively independent
> again. So lately I have experimented with
> saying goodnight and letting her put herself to
> bed.
>
> Two unfortunate things happened on different
> nights. Once she put her nightie on over her
> underwear, including the rather fierce corset
> she has to wear for her back's sake. I
> discovered this in the morning and she
> admitted she'd slept badly though she didn't
> know why. Another night she left her bedroom
> light on all night. I noticed it from my bedroom
> window when I was getting into bed myself but
> I assumed she'd got up for the toilet and
> dismissed it from my mind. But in the morning
> it was still on and she told me she'd wanted to
> get rid of it but couldn't. I can see she's going
> to be more peaceful and sleep better if I go back
> to tucking her up in bed and reading her Bible
> passage to her. I finish with her favourite
> prayer, 'The Lord bless you and keep you, the
> Lord make his face to shine upon you, the Lord
> lift up the light of his countenance upon you
> and give you his peace.' She seems to settle
> after this and, as far as I can tell, sleeps the
> night through. I have to admit that I take
> advantage of her difficulty in reading the clock
> now and sometimes say goodnight as early as

quarter to nine. This gives me a little time with Alan while Gavin is studying. I hope I'm not being selfish in this.

The time of her illness was, in fact, very peaceful. I wasn't sure that at her age she would come through it and I poured love around her. She was weak and floppy but a meek, biddable patient and when I left her at night I was not anxious. I had committed her into God's keeping and trusted him. I think there were only one or two nights at her lowest point when I decided to sleep in her bungalow in case she needed anything, but it proved unnecessary.

4
Energy without Capability

With the lighter evenings and a sense of spring in the air Mother was soon lively again. I didn't realise that returning strength combined with the early stages of senility would produce a terrible restlessness. But so it proved.

When she had first moved into the bungalow she had maintained, with her usual generosity of spirit, 'I'm not coming over to share your evening meal. The most precious time for husband and wife is when they are together again after work.' She agreed to Sunday lunch and, of course, she and I spent a lot of time together during the day but she was very firm about the early evening.

Now all this was thrown into the melting-pot. Because of her problems with kettles and finding things I prepared her tea about quarter to five and left her to eat it and watch television till I returned about 7.30 to sit with her up to her bedtime. But I soon found she couldn't sit still. She couldn't read the clock. She didn't know how long I'd been away and, like a small child since her illness, she needed desperately to run to 'Mummy'. She would appear at our back door by 6.00 most evenings just as Alan walked in the front. We welcomed her in, offered her some of our meal and let her spend the evening with us. But enough of her old sensitivity was still there to make her feel guilty. We had to reassure her constantly that it was all right. Alan was very patient but we both found this wearing. I wrote in my diary in late February:

> There are days when I feel Mother's clinginess smothering my life like a dark blanket, leaving no chink of freedom or relaxation. I must thank God that she's a loving soul, and has great faith. I know that as long as we all keep loving her she'll always respond warmly and gratefully to our love.

Little did I know then what I still had to face. It's *not* true that Alzheimer or dementia sufferers always respond with love and gratitude to kindness. Far from it. Nor is it always possible to know how to be kind in some situations. They have to be fed and taken to the toilet and put to bed. Trying to do these things can produce accusations of cruelty or, as Mother sometimes said later, which was really hurtful, 'I used to think you loved me.' But when that time came I was quite unprepared for it and had to learn agonisingly but, in the end thankfully, what it means to describe the love of God as boundless – literally without boundaries.

But to return to that spring of '86, what Mother suffered from most with her renewed energy was her inability to help me in any rational way. She had never been one to sit while anyone else was working. An entry at the end of February reads:

> I was washing up at her sink after we'd had our lunch together. She came rushing up. 'I must do that.' 'All right. I'll wash and you wipe.' She looked at the wet crockery and went towards the radiator where the tea-towel was hanging. But she stopped at the cutlery drawer, took up a spoon and came back. She looked at the wet things again and at the spoon

in her hand. She murmured, 'No, no, of course' and put the spoon away and brought a fork!

I tried to cope with this sort of thing by taking as little notice as possible so she wouldn't be upset, but as the days went on she was so physically rejuvenated that she began repulsing my help altogether. One Saturday in March she said, 'I'm not coming over interrupting your family, I'm having lunch here and painting a picture.' So I put out ham, tomatoes, crisps and some cooked vegetables in a bowl for her to warm up. When I came back later I asked her if she'd enjoyed her lunch. 'Oh yes, I had something,' she said. Later I found the bowl and the ham – with two bites out – in a china cupboard, the tomatoes in her fruit bowl and the crisps in a drawer. I wondered if she would eat at all if I didn't sit with her and make her. But if I insisted on doings things for her she said I was turning her into 'a horrid self-centred beast'.

On 14th March the diary says:

> Tonight she was having her usual jokey moan about my spoiling her. I filled her hot-water bottle and made her Horlicks. Suddenly she said, dead seriously, 'It's undermining my ego. Why do you do it?' I shrugged and laughed, really taken aback. She demanded, 'Why don't you answer? I never get an answer when I ask you this.' What could I say without undermining her ego even more? Yesterday she tried to drink the cold grey mixture in her cup without adding hot milk and I caught her attempting to fill her hot-water bottle with the whistle still on the kettle. I tried to explain this gently. 'Honestly, I'm not looking for work,' I said, 'only you might have been badly scalded.' But it was so sad. She became low and weepy

and spoke as if we'd been quarrelling. 'We'll call it a truce,' she said.

I remember it had been a specially uplifting day till then, with a Christian Coffee Morning and talk in the Moot Hall, followed by a Lent lunch and ecumenical prayers. In the afternoon was my Lent Course which Mother attended too. She really entered into it all and loved the people, the Bible study and chatting over a cup of tea afterwards. Again I can understand with hindsight that physical tiredness in the evenings affected her mental state but I remember well how hurt and bewildered I felt when I went back to my house that night. I concluded the diary entry, 'I can only pray for her and myself.'

It was the first real sign of a change in her personality and I wasn't able to find comfort when I felt my genuine love had not been appreciated. I wasn't recognising yet that she was not in her right mind. What must be the grief of our Lord when his children who are in full possession of their faculties turn away and reject him? No human soul can comprehend that.

We had some days of real warmth in late March and she became much more cheerful. This brightness seemed to indicate a genuine increase in her mental alertness, and I really thought she was getting better. A former neighbour from Newcastle came to visit one afternoon and Mother was very jolly with her and sounded just like her old self. I tried allowing her to put herself to bed that evening – after I'd filled her hot-water bottle and seen her drink her Horlicks. It worked! And for a while she was up and dressed in the mornings when I went round, sometimes a little oddly, but the small trouble of rectifying this was more than offset by her gain in self-respect. Even her art improved, though she often dipped her pencil in the water-pot without noticing anything odd about it.

I'm sure it was in the mercy of God that we had this period of blessed respite. There were still scattered moments of confusion but they seemed less wounding to her ego. On 18th March, for example, I wrote:

> Today I found her tugging hard at one of the sink taps. When I asked what she was trying to do she said, 'Well, if I could get it off it would be much easier to dry it up.' Oh joy! She joined in my merriment when she realised what 'it' was. Spontaneously laughing together was just like the old days. Thank God for it!

There was a setback during a cold wet spell in April. I see now how much her condition was affected by the weather. She always loved light and warmth and her whole being was revived by it. But on 17th April I wrote:

> Alan woke me at 5.30am to say the phone was ringing. She must be ill! I was out of bed instantly and into shoes and a dressing gown and ran over. She greeted me in the hall with an outdoor coat over her underwear. 'Are you poorly?' I asked. 'No,' she said, 'I'm all right. It was you I was worried about. I hadn't heard from you since you went over. I kept thinking you must have slipped.' I realised she thought it was early evening. She said she had been over to our house twice and rung up twice. I let her talk so her anxiety could come out. It had been pouring when I said goodnight last night and I remember saying, 'I'll run quickly.' She must have had an anxiety dream and woken perhaps as early as three or four in the morning, and thought I ought to be coming back soon. It took me a long time to convince her what time it really was and then she

became quite worried about herself and said she would pray about this confusion. I don't think I was as kind or helpful as I should have been.

What was new was her own awareness of confusion. There were very few occasions when she put such worries into words so it's hard to say how conscious she was of it most of the time. I think she forgot these lapses as soon as they happened and so went on thinking she was perfectly capable and in charge of her life.

But that summer of 1986 she had something fresh to occupy her mind. Her older sister was to pay us a visit. Despite Mother's frequent forgetfulness over small things this began now to dominate her thoughts, and though I knew she would scarcely be capable of looking after Aunty Flo in any meaningful sense, her own view of her personal responsibility was quite different!

5
A Visit from Aunty

The next few weeks before Aunty's visit were full of 'When Flo comes . . .' Everything had to be perfect. 'Is the boy going to cut the grass for Flo coming?' was a daily anxiety.

The niece in Surrey who looked after Aunty Flo was taking her family to Devon for a three-week holiday. When she had phoned me in the winter to ask if we could have Aunty for those dates it had already been planned that in the middle week our family would look after Mother while Alan and I went camping in the Scottish Highlands. This, I must make clear, was at their insistence and they had organised their own time off to do it for us. Fortunately they said they were perfectly happy to take on Aunty as well. She would sleep in the second bedroom in Mother's bungalow but they knew they would have to see to all meals and make sure the old ladies were tucked up at night. As Aunty was then ninety-three this was quite an undertaking.

I reckoned that as I had one week of her visit first I would be able to see what problems there might be before Alan and I left the young to cope. One small tension was created by Mother thinking Aunty was eating too much. She kept urging me to give her less. This was so unlike her that it was really odd, but maybe the sight of someone older than herself with a good appetite was now offensive to her.

Another thing that bothered Mother was that Aunty talked little. She answered, if at all, slowly and deliberately but briefly. Aunty had always been a self-contained person with precise views. I think talking was quite an effort for her now and as her mind was reasonably clear she probably found Mother's inconsequential or repetitive remarks very irritating. I noticed too that Mother was a little jealous of any time I spent with Aunty after she herself was in bed. It is a sad truth that the old can become small and petty in their relationships, like little children.

But mostly Mother and Aunty enjoyed each other's company and I had time to prepare for our camping holiday and for Helen and Claire coming to share duties with Katherine, Mark and Gavin. The young folk organised a sensible rota. As it was the girls who had the bedtime and early morning duties of dressing and undressing – insofar as they needed to help – the boys had other tasks, helping with meals and driving the old ladies about. Helen brought her daughter, Clare, whose presence delighted her great-grandma and great-great-aunt. Helen's and Claire's husbands – if my memory serves me right – visited once or twice too.

When Alan and I drove north and found our first camping spot in a remote glen in Angus I found it almost impossible to believe I had no one to look after. It took me at least twenty-four hours to grow accustomed to the freedom. Of course we phoned home several times. Once Helen sounded quite upset because Aunty Flo had told them it was her birthday that day but too late for them to go out and buy a card or bake a cake. I was surprised, because I knew her birthday was in October and in fact that day was the birthday of another sister, Aunty Madeline, who had died about ten years before. It was one of the few instances of confusion in Aunty Flo.

One funny incident happened which they didn't tell us about till later. Mother had woken at 1am and imagined it was time for Aunty's morning tea. As this was the girls' job and she had at last realised that making it herself was beyond her, she had gone out in a coat over her nightie but lost her bearings in the dark and rung a neighbour's doorbell. The neighbour is a very caring, practical widow, living alone. She came to our house and managed to rouse Helen and Claire. They all ended up together in Mother's bungalow drinking tea before they got the old folks back to bed.

Helen said afterwards she'd have put up with being roused in the middle of the night but she resented Mother saying, 'I won't hold it against you, darling. I know young people need their sleep and find it hard to get up. I won't tell your mother about it.' The irony was that Mother had almost certainly woken Aunty and created the situation herself. After that Aunty put the sneck on the front door at night, after the girls left, to deter Mother. When I came home I saved her this trouble for her remaining week's stay by putting it on myself and going out of the back door, taking that key with me. It seemed to work because we had no more night wandering.

But this situation, where their sweet-natured Grandma could hurt the family's feelings, was totally new and very disconcerting. Fortunately they could all discuss it and try to laugh it off at the end of the day, and daughter Claire, as a young social worker, already had some experience of the confused elderly and could put these misunderstandings in context. But such things are never quite believable from someone close to you whom you've loved and respected all your life.

We wanted Mother to have a holiday too because we felt a change of scenery would stimulate her. It was booked for the day Aunty was to leave us. So there was a hilarious hour when the niece, her husband, her two boys, her brother, his wife and baby and her father, Mother's youngest brother, now about eighty, all came up north in a minibus and arrived at 4.30. The boys had a mad rush about our garden to let off steam and everyone was fed a scratch tea of bread and jam and biscuits. When they felt ready for the journey back we packed Aunty into the minibus with them and managed to set off ourselves for Galloway within a few minutes of their leaving.

Mother found the swift change from 'looking after Flo' as she put it to being in a strange place very bewildering. But in a day or two she perked up and insisted on helping with meals. One day she said, 'I don't seem to be doing this very well' and I found she was trying to peel a carrot with another carrot! The good thing was that her appetite improved and once she asserted, 'I ate as much as Aunty Flo, didn't I?'

For her age she still had amazing stamina. A beach nearby was down a really long flight of steps. I thought she might stay in the car but she came gamely down and sat among the rocks, and managed the climb back with only a short rest on a seat. Her paintings were deteriorating however. Once she turned the sketch-pad round and continued on the picture upside down. She spoke of being 'humiliated' by her failures which grieved me very much and I wished she would give up, but she had always used holidays as an opportunity to sketch landscapes and she wasn't ready to stop trying.

One day I tested her memory because Uncle had said Aunty Flo couldn't name the Prime Minister. At her great age I think Aunty was indifferent to current politics or perhaps was just mischievously not co-operating. Anyway I was pleased to find that Mother could say 'Mrs Thatcher' after a moment's struggling for the name.

But when we were home again Mother expected to find Aunty Flo there and as the sun was warm she said, 'I'm sure Aunty would like to sit out in the garden.' She seemed annoyed when I couldn't produce her and for some weeks more she still spoke as if Aunty was there and always called the spare bedroom 'Flo's room'.

But the memories of Aunty's visit faded with the summer and cooler, darker days brought with them more distressing changes and a greater challenge to my understanding of God's lesson of love.

6
Shocks and Anxieties

The entry for 28th October 1986 reads:

> Yesterday the unbelievable happened. Mother used the linen basket as the toilet and then must have tried to dispose of the result in the kitchen waste bucket using one of her spencers. I found her in a bemused way trying to wash out the spencer in the sink. 'I can't bear anything dirty,'; 'I don't understand what's happened,'; 'I must get to the bottom of this' were some of the things she said over and over again.
>
> I was desperately sorry for her and prayed to be wise in my handling of the situation. When she pressed me on what had happened I just told her in a very matter-of-fact voice that she'd got a bit confused about where the toilet was and not to worry, it would probably never happen again, and to forget all about it. She was very anxious and low and said, 'If Alan or anyone ever found out about this I'd never be able to live here again.' This was her strongest expression of distress and suggested she had a good idea what had happened but couldn't put it into words. However, as soon as cleanliness reigned again she perked up a little.

At lunch she said, 'I don't know if I can eat anything.' But she did try. When I said I'd make a cup of tea she said, 'That sounds better. That should be clean anyway.' I had whisked her washing away to my machine and hoped Art Club that afternoon would be a distraction. Glimmerings of memory returned as we re-entered the house afterwards. 'What happened this morning?' she asked. 'Something made me sad.' I told her she often felt sad if she couldn't manage things and it was best just to remember the happy times. Tea in front of the fire and television helped her to forget. I really think her mind refused to grasp it. It was a sort of nebulous horror which she felt involved in but for which she was not responsible.

Another mysterious anxiety took hold of her that autumn: a fear that she would have to go down the hill at night. We live on a fairly steep hill and maybe it stemmed from the night she wandered out when I was away. For many weeks she spoke half-finished sentences at bedtime. 'I suppose I'll have to go down the –' or 'I'll have to get into bed down the –.' When I reassured her that she was going to be here cosy in her own bed she would say, 'But I will have to go down the hill sometime I suppose,' or more hopefully 'So I don't have to go down the hill?'

There were two more 'accidents' before Christmas – each time in the early hours of a Monday morning, the day we went to Art Club. Was it an anxiety thing? I didn't make that connection in my diary because after the first time she appeared unconcerned and when I cleared up she just remarked, 'I could do that.' I had noticed her laughing at herself sometimes about not knowing 'where to go for that'. If she was walking about restlessly I would suggest she might need the loo. Once she looked into the bathroom and said, 'Well, I've got that one ready you see but I think there's another one.' I told her very emphatically that she only had one and she shrugged her shoulders. 'Well, I think you're wrong,' she said, 'but still . . .'

An even more astonishing confusion showed up at church, which showed that I was still unable to grasp that anyone could forget lifelong habits. On 30th November the diary entry reads:

> Today Mother received the wafer at Communion and didn't know what to do with it. I tried to jog her arm to indicate she should lift her hands to her mouth but she didn't. As the curate approached with the cup she transferred the wafer to her left hand. With great presence of mind he took it from her and put it into her mouth. Then she was able to take the cup. Fortunately she seemed to forget the incident at once and suffered no embarrassment.

But the diary records that the next two Sundays she was similarly confused. I felt acutely that she was causing a disturbance at the most solemn moment of the service and perhaps upsetting those around her. So I made it a matter of earnest prayer that she would know what to do next time and after only the slightest hesitation she lifted the wafer to her mouth correctly. On Christmas Day she did so again. The following Sunday she held up her hands in a praying attitude but I was able to show her gently what to do and she ate the wafer. I have no doubt now that prayer about these things helped not only her but my own attitude to her problems. When I brought something to the Lord I felt the wonderful blessing of sharing which we experience when we talk to a friend about a problem. The act of sharing is always a relief but in sharing with Jesus I could feel the power of his love shedding peace and serenity in my heart. As I approached the Communion rail in this spirit I was no longer tense and maybe this communicated itself to Mother too, so that her own anxiety and confusion fell away. It is impossible to overestimate the power of prayer.

Mother had been coming with us to the Abbey twice every Sunday – on foot in the morning, by car in the evening when we knew the walk back up the hill would be more tiring – but on 15th December it was bitterly cold and frosty. Mark, who had to leave for his train – he was coming home at weekends at that time – offered to stay in with her till train time which would be about quarter of an hour before we would be home. He sat with her for *Songs of Praise* but she was very restless and kept saying, 'I know they have to have little jaunts on their own.' He reminded her we were at Evensong, so she said sadly, 'But they know I love to go to church,' and when he mentioned the bitter weather she said, 'I don't mind the cold. I haven't been cold at all today, anyway.' She had, of course. She felt the cold terribly. But she was so restless he felt unable to leave her till we returned.

Anxieties were becoming obsessive. As Christmas approached I couldn't convince her that all her presents were wrapped and labelled. Even on Christmas Eve when I kissed her goodnight and said, 'See you on Christmas morning,' she said, 'Yes, and I must get everyone's presents ready.' I told her I was taking them all over in a carrier bag, except Mark's which were two new bike tyres. I'd left these in her spare room because the shape was a give-away. I explained this several times and showed her them again and again, till she protested, 'Of course I see that, I'm not stupid.' Still on Christmas morning she said, 'I've found a funny thing on Flo's bed.'

We let her think she was joining in the games on Christmas afternoon but even when we wrote a definition down for her in *Call My Bluff* she couldn't repeat it. Still she seemed happy, especially with Helen's new baby, Daniel, and, by the grace of God I'm sure, no upsets marred the joyful day.

On January 4th the diary records:

> Yesterday was the first time Katherine had seen Mother tear something up. She calmly tore in two the cover of the new *Radio Times*. When I showed her what it was she said, 'Oh well, there's no *Radio Times* on that part.' There was some logic in this as no programme pages were damaged but Katherine was dismayed to see she was quite unrepentant – it was so out of character.

The same evening I felt touched to the quick. I had gently encouraged Mother to go round the bed and be close to the fire for undressing and she said, 'Thank you for speaking so kindly to me.' It made me realise how often we must all be pointing out her mistakes and telling her what to do and what not to do and how an edge of exasperation must creep into our voices. I noted, 'With God's help we must have in our hearts the true love which will make such impatience an impossibility.'

Each phase of dementia has its own problems and this time was perhaps the hardest for Mother. She could still read, write and speak with some coherence, especially in company, but she was also doing so many odd things where she had to be restrained that she must have felt she was the constant butt of comment and criticism, however well-meant. In the cold weather I gave her two hot-water bottles and one night when I had filled one and was putting it in her bed she poured her Horlicks into the other and I found her trying to drink out of it. I felt she was getting more difficult and argumentative but I see now that confusion was so undermining her that while she could still find words she had to assert herself.

Fortunately keeping the diary helped me to find some of her answers funny as well as poignant and I wrote them down straightaway. There was the time when she wanted to put her coat and hat on to go to Art Club an hour before it was time. She finally gave in and pointed to one of her own paintings on the wall – a lovely one of trees – and said, 'Well, I have to live with *them*, haven't I?'

I longed to stop taking her to the Art Club. We gave a lift to a lady who was six months older than Mother and who could still draw beautifully. Mother seemed unaware of this sometimes but occasionally she grew almost fractious about her own inability and I was grieved for her and for those who sat near her, though everyone was full of kindliness and sympathy. Luckily that January was so snowy that meetings were cancelled and before they resumed God showed me how to get out of the difficulty even when I had not yet made it a specific matter of prayer.

7
Is She a Different Person?

After church on the Sunday before we were to go back to the Art Club a friend caught me and asked if there was any afternoon when Mother could come to tea. It entered my mind at once that here was my godsent opportunity. 'Would tomorrow be all right?' I asked and as she agreed I turned to Mother to draw her into the conversation. 'You were thinking of not bothering with art any more, weren't you?' She nodded happily. It all happened so simply. Next day I took her and left her at the friend's house and when I went to collect her I heard her laughing with her hostess and two other friends in the most natural and delightful way. What a joy! She hadn't laughed like that for ages.

Once the principle was accepted that I went to Art Club alone I made arrangements with a neighbour's daughter who worked for Crossroads to come in on Monday afternoons. She brought her three-year-old son with her and Mother loved this. I even felt bold enough to show her what I had been painting. She admired it and said, 'Well, I haven't got going yet.' But she didn't seem troubled. I recorded in the diary that deep down perhaps she was relieved to have the decision to stop painting taken out of her hands. Certainly the extra company acted as a stimulus and I don't think she made as many odd remarks to other people as she did to me.

Still, the snippets of dialogue that I recorded in my diary show how her grasp of reality was slipping, or rather how different realities became mixed up in her mind. 'Have you got a book there to read?' I asked one morning when I had some letters to write. She held up the cover on the chair arm. 'I've got this.' 'I know, pet,' I said, 'but have you got a book to read?' 'Well, I can read this,' and she studied its plain buff surface. After lunch I said, 'Drink up your tea.' 'I am,' she said, picking up a book and tilting it to her mouth.

Television was similarly mixed up with everything else. 'You haven't eaten your segments of tangerine,' I said, coming back to her one evening. She stroked her fingers. 'I had all these.' Then she looked at the television screen where Jonathan Miller was talking with Terry Wogan. 'And everything he's been saying, too.'

Sometimes she picked up on newspaper headlines. Our help had phoned to say she had a chance of going to Spain for three weeks as someone in their church party was ill, and could she come tomorrow instead of her usual day? Mother was thrilled to know she was coming tomorrow as she loved her visits, but then she saw in the paper 'Three die in plane crash.' 'Oh dear,' she said, 'I hope it wasn't Mrs Stobbart.' I reassured her, but she turned a page and said, 'I don't know what this refers to. Some sort of accident. I don't know if that's Mrs Stobbart's lot.' This time the headline was 'Secret Accident Test' – about nuclear weapons.

In the February diary toilet problems and general restlessness loom over everything else. She seemed not to link the sensations of needing to go with what she actually had to do to avoid accidents. This was very trying for us both but there was an even sadder side to her restlessness which I think I understand more now than I did at the time. As I am older myself now, having reached my threescore years and ten, I realise how like I am in many ways to Mother. I am hopeless at doing nothing. I knit, sew or do the ironing if I am watching television. I even knit if I'm reading a book. Though I spend a few hours most days at my word processor I have very active spells in between – doing gardening, housework, shopping or out walking with Alan, and from time to time entertaining family and playing with grandchildren. I never have nothing to do.

Re-reading my diary I try to put myself in Mother's position. She was still physically fit at eighty-seven, with corresponding energy. But because of her memory problems there was almost nothing she could do to exercise the faculties she had left. Old skills like painting, cooking, gardening, sewing and knitting were now a mystery. If she attempted them she had no idea how to proceed to achieve anything at all. Even eating was a skill she was rapidly losing. I often had to feed her to get her to take anything. We had many conversations on the lines of 'Anything you need, darling?' when she got up and wandered round her sitting-room. 'Well, I hardly know. I was just looking for . . .' (all names were impossible now). 'Would you like the radio on?' 'Well, that's the question. I'm willing to do anything I have to.'

How I wish now that I had spent more time just sitting with her lovingly, perhaps reading the Bible which she always enjoyed, or praying together or chatting about old times! She literally did not know how to occupy the time, and for one who had led so active a life it must have been desperately frustrating. No wonder she was so restless and occasionally tore up books and papers.

There is a tendency, when someone close to you is becoming irrational, to arrive belatedly at a moment when you accept they are not the person they were. But this is a dangerous moment. At last you feel you can stop struggling to keep up a pretence that the old relationship can be maintained. Your new duties are clear: you must take over all the physical caring and just be thankful to see your patient clean and quiet between whiles so you can get on with the rest of your responsibilities. I know there must have been many days when I felt like this about Mother. Yet I knew from our bedtime Bible reading and prayers that her spirit was still reachable. After all, the immortal part of us, however veiled by dementia, cannot itself be touched by what is happening to the chemistry of the brain. The person you knew and loved is still there, somewhere, despite the changes, and needs you probably more desperately than ever before. When I think of this I yearn for my time over again to do better.

I always kissed Mother goodnight but I regret now that I didn't show her more demonstrative love during all the daylight hours. I never outwardly lost my temper but that is a poor, negative claim to make. Mostly I was gentle and kindly but that too was not the same as glowing with the true love of God. Do we ever pray enough in these situations? Do we ever draw as we should on the eternal fountain of his love? I'm afraid not. I could have surrounded Mother with a more pure, more joyful and more constant love than I did.

The lesson God was showing me at the beginning of this testing period was to learn what LOVE in capital letters truly means. I believe I saw it in flashes rather than in a sustained brilliant light. But what I can witness to with thankfulness is that whenever I earnestly sought his help he was there with me, true to his word: 'If with all your heart you truly seek me, you will ever surely find me.'

8

Her Self-Respect – My Pride

Probably the saddest loss that dementia brings eventually is that of speech. In spring '87 Mother could still talk but she rarely used anyone's name. My family were 'the boys' or 'the girls' and Helen's children were 'the little ones'.

But in the diary entry for 13th March I noted:

> She hardly uses even common nouns at all. I thought I would try out on a little walk today asking her the names of things. I pointed out to her a car, a gate, a wall, a wheel, a crocus, a snowdrop, a van, a motorbike. Not one could she name. But I was interested that she could say 'steps' when we came to them. I thought, yes, that's related to the verb 'to step' and she's doing the action as she goes up them so it's very real to her. But unconnected names are just sounds plucked out of the air. It must be significant too that the first words babies learn are nouns, and, just as the first leaves of spring are usually the first to fall, so nouns drop first out of the memory of old age. We were laughing and good-humoured all the time we were out, probably because it was a bright mild day, so I kept up the little game by asking her what the key was when I opened her front door. 'Oh, it's one of those things,' she said. 'Well, what's its purpose in life?' I asked. 'To look after me,' she said quite seriously.

I hope I wasn't undermining her self-respect in playing these little games. I had no conception at all that language would eventually go altogether. All I wanted was for her to hang on to names so she wouldn't feel frustrated.

A few days later she picked up the tea cosy and asked, 'What's this?' 'Just the tea cosy,' I said. She looked at it hard and then said, 'But it's also "Lord, in thy mercy, hear our prayer" and I've known it for years.' We had just been to the Lent Group and I suppose the phrase was running in her head, but it showed that spiritual matters had a stronger reality than the objects around her. I wish I'd taken more notice of that fact at the time.

Although her own speech was deteriorating Mother understood very well what was said to her and could feel hurt or resentful. This was where her self-respect could be seriously damaged. One day in early April this was brought home to me very strongly. We were watching England in a rugby match on television, Alan, Mark, Gavin and myself. I went to bring Mother over as I often did on a Saturday afternoon so she would have company and a change of scene. She sat on the settee, opposite the gas-fire, but our house was never as warm as her bungalow and she began pulling her cardigan round her. When I asked her if she was cold she admitted she was, so I fetched a rug and tucked her up tight. A few minutes later she began gasping and throwing it off. I said, in a bit of a grumbly voice I expect, 'You complained of being cold. I've only just covered you up.' She pointed to the rugby players on the screen and said, 'They don't have to be told what to do all the time.'

That night I really thought about the many other times when we must have pained her in this way. I felt I had had a bad day with her and I laid it before the Lord. I wasn't so much repenting of my irritation as just wordlessly wanting his help, needing to be close to him.

First, as ever, came the word LOVE. This time was added the thought, 'in the present moment'. I turned this around in my mind a little and thought, yes, when else can you show love but here and now? The past is already a lost opportunity and the future – even of the next minute – is still to come. It has to be now. Obvious, I felt like telling God. But I knew he wanted me to think about it particularly in connection with Mother. And then it hit me. The present moment is all there is for a dementia sufferer. Maybe the far past still echoes around but the immediate past is dead.

Now I began to realise what it must be like for Mother. Yes, I thought, she is very much alive in each present, isolated minute but her self-respect is peculiarly vulnerable, because, without memory, she is also trapped there. She has no idea what she has just done or what has been said to her a few moments before. So why do I try to justify my present actions to her? I feel hurt, I suppose, I told God.

Immediately I knew he was asking me a simple question, 'What is hurt but your pride?' And again the word, '*All* you need is love for each new moment.'

My pride! Of course, it was my pride that was hurt. But what did I want with that? What use was it? Far from being useful it was positively harmful. It was getting in the way of that love I kept praying for. How could I be filled with love by the action of the Holy Spirit if I didn't empty myself first? And what was filling me up to the brim? Pride and resentment.

As I knelt there it was as if a huge burden lifted off me. No pride, just love. How many of our thoughts, words and actions are activated by pride! On the global scene, how many wars! Rid ourselves of that and our whole attitude to life is transformed. No wonder Jesus said, 'Blessed are the meek.'

I rose from my knees that night with a great sense of release. My pride, which had loomed so large and been so wounded by what felt like the pin-pricks of a thousand tiny injustices, became a heap of dust which a breath of his Spirit blew away in a moment. I think I truly understood then what it means to say, 'His service is perfect freedom.' Freedom from pride brings freedom from resentment, from irritation, from frustration, and it leads to the great freedom – to love.

By contrast, the world's idea of freedom is a miserable one. The world would have encouraged me to find freedom from Mother, from duty, from responsibility, so that I could be free to 'do my own thing'. And any relief or even happiness I might have felt would have been as ephemeral as a will-o'-the-wisp. God's freedoms from and freedoms to are openings to heaven.

But, sadly, as I kept finding, it is one thing to learn a lesson and another to hold on to it in more testing situations. As Mother's personality changed even more I had to keep relearning that lesson in the days to come.

9

Downward Steps

At the end of April some good friends of long standing came to visit us. It was also seven years to the day since my sister had died. Strangely, that morning Mother said, 'I keep thinking about Janet. How is it I don't see anything of her these days?' I was surprised and delighted that she could say her name – the thought must have come into her own mind through some mysterious association of the time. She certainly didn't know what date it was. I said, 'Janet died seven years ago, darling.' She said, 'Yes, I know, but still . . . ' I told her she would see Janet in the Kingdom and she said vaguely, 'Well, I hope so.'

Mother (aged 75) with Janet

When she was at tea with us and our visitors it was the first time that she ever admitted to someone's face that she didn't know who they were. She said, 'Who is that gentleman who's smiling at me?' She had known him for forty-one years though it was a year or more since their last visit. They were shocked by the change in her, yet she was bright and smiling with them all the time, only she ate almost nothing.

Feeding and toilet problems were becoming acute. With the latter I had occasional help and advice from the district nurse but the mechanics of eating were now so difficult that it was embarrassing to have anyone outside the family at table with her. She couldn't manage a knife and fork at all so I cut her food up small and gave her a spoon, but usually she used her fingers, like a small child – if she would eat at all. One day she tried picking up stewed apple and custard. I pointed out her spoon and she said, 'That's all right,' and carried on with her fingers, dropping blobs of custard down her front. As gently as I could I said, 'You see, that's why people use spoons.' She seemed quite irritated. 'I don't know why you keep saying things. I'll do it any way you tell me to,' and she continued to dabble in the custard. 'But you get your fingers all messy.' 'There's no question of being messy at all,' she pronounced firmly.

It was in little scenes like this that the changes in her personality began to show themselves. How far was she aware, I wonder now, of the lack of cleanliness in her habits, she who had had from her nursing training a lifelong devotion to hygiene. That spring and summer she moved from the assertive denial of it that I saw in that little episode to a weepy bewilderment about it, particularly over toilet problems. I should point out again that there was nothing the matter with her physically. She could often go five hours without needing the toilet. The loss of connections was all in the brain. And though she sometimes said, 'You needn't go away' when I left her in the bathroom I think there was still a deep psychological resistance to the involvement of another person in this private function, which might account for the protest she usually made about going at all. Born in Victorian times, she had been brought up to standards of strict modesty. Today many people would call it prudery.

But even this was beginning to change, as a funny incident showed one day when we took her out for a picnic in May. Her balance was now not quite as good as it had been and she had less confidence over rough ground, stiles or footbridges where she clung to me and the handrail. A related trouble was that she suffered from car sickness. Now that she was rather hunched and bent she couldn't lean back on the seat and was therefore not fully supported. That day I unfastened the hook and eye of her skirt to ease her and completely forgot when we arrived at our picnic place. Next moment I noticed her skirt gently slithering down round her ankles. I'm afraid I dissolved in helpless mirth and so did the family, though they tried to turn away and hide it. Happily, she seemed not in the least offended, as if there was nothing strange in my sorting her clothing in a public place with two of her grandchildren, Katherine and Gavin, in full view.

It was on that same picnic that she gave us another cause of merriment which she couldn't share but which seemed to give her no offence. She picked up *Joseph Andrews*, one of Gavin's A Level set books, and read aloud over and over again, 'Joseph and his dog'. Gavin, who was trying to learn quotes from *King Lear* and *Antony and Cleopatra*, was very puzzled by this phrase and at last took the book from her and read amidst great hilarity, 'Joseph and his dogged persistence in virtue'. There was no way we could explain to her what was funny or that we were not laughing at her, but fortunately she smiled too. She was aware that those around her were relaxed and happy, something she always loved to see. Thankfully, she had not as yet descended into the real night of senility.

The joy of reading, however, as this incident showed, had been taken from her. Though she recognised words she could retain nothing of their meaning, so I bought her two picture books about the royal family and one of the soap opera, *Coronation Street*, which she had watched on and off for years. There was very little text in any of them and she seemed to get some pleasure from turning the pages and pointing and saying, 'Oh that's – you know –.' Sometimes I could leave her alone for as much as an hour without her fretting too much. This was a great – if temporary – relief.

I was really sorry that it was getting harder to arrange company for her, but experiences of taking her anywhere were becoming very painful. She still liked to be with people and she had always enjoyed an evening we spent with a Christian group once a month at the Diocesan Retreat House where we had dinner followed by a talk. We went for the last time on 5th June 1987. I couldn't get her to eat the starter and she was holding up the meal for everyone else at our table. In desperation I spooned the grapefruit pieces to her and she said out loud, 'That gentleman's watching me.' Although I knew everyone well and they were all very sweet towards Mother I don't think they realised how senile she had become. I was so used to her eating problems that I had forgotten it would be embarrassing for others to sit round while one adult fed another adult. She had also reached the stage of trying to eat the pattern on her plate. At home we always gave her plain ones. Although she could still smile sweetly at people and even reply to questions I think that was the day when it really came home to me that such public occasions must come to an end. It was another sad landmark on the downward path.

10
Her Last Holiday

Later that summer we also realised that we could never again take Mother away to a strange house. I will never forget our last visit with her to Galloway. The cottage was an old stone one well off a quiet road north of Gatehouse of Fleet. There was a downstairs bedroom for her and the bathroom was close by on the same level. We thought this was ideal but we hadn't reckoned with her increasing confusion about things and places.

The worst happened on the Wednesday night. She had got up twice after I'd put her to bed which was most unusual and I should have realised that all was not well. Then Katherine heard her wandering about in the night and went down to help her back into bed. When she had got her settled she switched on the bedside lamp and stood it on the floor so that if Mother got up again she wouldn't fall.

In the morning I found a disaster had occurred. Mother must have imagined that the lamp was the toilet as the shade was large and white. Unfortunately she had stood in the result, then wandered about the room and touched things with soiled hands. There were two beds in the room and both duvets as well as books, the Bible by her bed, the lamp itself and her nightie, dressing-gown and bedsocks, all had to be cleaned. I put on the immersion heater and the hot rail in the bathroom. Alan carted away things for the washing-machine and I managed with great difficulty to get a poor little shivering Mother into the bath. 'I've never known anything like this in my life before,' she said. Luckily the day was sunny and we laid things outside to dry, but it took us until eleven o'clock to get all cleaned and Mother breakfasted.

Then Katherine suggested Alan and I should go out for a quiet picnic on our own and she and Gavin would give Grandma lunch and take her out in the other car if it stayed fine. They even made the picnic for us while we were hesitating and filled flasks and forgot nothing. So we drove off, unencumbered as birds, over the hill road to Creetown and along the estuary to a seat by the water where we watched the tide come flooding up Wigtown Bay till it bobbed a little blue rowing-boat moored just by the shore ten yards away.

By then we felt we had had our two hours of peace and beauty and we drove back to find a note saying where they had taken Grandma and we joined them at Mossyard beach about seven miles from the cottage. Several families came to the beach and this gave Mother great delight watching the small children playing in the sand. Blessedly she had no recollection of what had happened in the morning. I was thankful to see her experiencing positive pleasure and I took her arm to exercise her along the beach to keep her circulation going, but all at once – as so often – she became bewildered by the commonest thing. As we walked by the incoming tide a wave lapped nearly to her feet. 'Oh, I don't know about that,' she cried. 'I don't think I want that.'

This is the difficulty with anyone at that stage of senility. Ordinary, everyday things can suddenly become frightening and yet there can still be benefit and stimulus from changes in surroundings. I'm sure the sea air did Mother good both physically and mentally. After the Wednesday night she slept well and was very serene on our last evening and agreed with me that she'd enjoyed the holiday. But the first few days she had been restless and talked wildly. Once I had said, 'Why not sit in front of the fire? You're cold and I can't look after you if you won't keep warm.' She said, 'You don't have to look after me. My mother does that, very well.' Senility is often called 'second childhood' and if it was her own mother she was thinking of I was very glad because my Grandmother was a delightful character with a sweet sense of humour who lived to be eighty-nine in full possession of her faculties. But this was the dilemma. Mother could behave like two different people in a short space of time. One moment you would have said she was perfectly safe to take anywhere and it would be cruel to deprive her of the pleasure, the next you would feel she was in need of full-time nursing care.

Although it had ended better than we had hoped Alan and I both felt we wouldn't feel brave enough to risk taking her away with us again. We couldn't expect Katherine to come another year to help us out. We suspected she might be a newly-married bride by then. Mark, busy with his career in computing and Gavin, who would now be going to university, had their own friends with whom they wanted to go away and in any event Mother wouldn't have tolerated one of them helping with the toilet.

However, all the family felt that Alan and I should have a break on our own before the summer ended. Alan's demanding job – he was Director of Planning for the District Council – meant that he didn't like to be away from the office for very long at a time, but we were persuaded to take eleven days, which included two weekends so that we could travel a fair distance. Claire took some of her annual leave and Helen brought her two children with her to stay in our house. I am still thankful that none of the family felt that their helpless old Grandma was not their business. They all loved her dearly and there was never any thought that she should be shoved away out of their lives now that she had become what the world would call a trial or a liability. There was also loving concern for my need, as the principal carer, to have a brief period of respite.

I have to confess that the thought of a camping tour with Alan in our beloved highlands and islands thrilled me very much but before we went we sorted out more practical forms of help for Mother.

For example, the Practice Sister had suggested a platform to facilitate getting Mother into the bath and this was delivered by Social Services and a handle was fitted on the wall. Since eating proper meals was now virtually beyond her I bought lots of concentrated invalid foods and baby meals which were a little more successful. I also began to put her into incontinence pads if we were going out anywhere. I was still having my neighbour's daughter from Crossroads regularly once a week for two hours and my good Mrs Stobbart still came both to clean and sit in as a friend. As our family declared they had truly enjoyed being together the last time when they had looked after both Mother and Aunty Flo I felt able to leave them in charge with a good conscience.

11

Abandoned

The first words I recorded in the journal of our holiday were 'Mother's poor little face with its yearning look is still with me. "You won't be gone too long, will you?" she said. Mrs Stobbart looked up brightly and tried to take her attention with the 'royal' book. Alan and I backed out smiling.'

I tried hard to shed any feeling of guilt and was much cheered next day after a phone call home. Katherine reported that Mother's face had lighted up when she saw Daniel, Helen's baby, now ten months old.

It was as well that we didn't know some of what went on or we could not have enjoyed our holiday so much. Later in the week my phone calls elicited the admission that Mother was asking when I would be back but the family was managing to reassure her. It wasn't until I read the horrifically honest diary the girls had kept that I appreciated what they and Mother had been through.

The worst problem had been Mother's constipation. Worried about her internal state after several days they had called the surgery and a nurse had been sent to give her an enema. Unfortunately the nurse was a man. Mother had been terribly upset and all three of the girls tried to calm her but he was still unable to do anything because she was so tense. She kept crying, 'Lord, have mercy' and trying to stop him with her hand. The girls were very distressed for her. Since his visit was virtually a failure the girls did what they could with a very laxative diet which he recommended. Either that, their diary says, or the fact that Mark had been praying, produced results in a rather drastic way when Katherine was on duty alone. She phoned urgently from the bungalow for help and Helen and Claire ran along to find the bathroom in rather the state Mother's bedroom had been at the Galloway cottage. But Mother refused absolutely to go in the bath. They wondered if they could lift her in bodily but she was so resistant that they gave up for fear of hurting her and washed her where she stood. She said, 'I'm not an animal' and 'If my mother was here that wouldn't happen' but at last they got her dressed and into the living room with the fire full on and she eventually calmed down.

She remained very difficult about food and when they tried to coax her she would say, 'I want to eat but you see I just can't.' Sometimes she referred to me by name. 'Is there any reason why I can't see Prue?' At other times it seemed as if she confused me with her mother. A note in Katherine's writing on the third day says, 'Grandma refers to Mum as "my mother".'

One evening she was more cheerful and enjoyed Aled Jones, the chorister, singing hymns on the television. She even asked Claire about her job and admired her 'quick way of giving her instructions'. She was still bright next morning when Katherine took early duty but as soon as breakfast appeared she became fractious and Katherine wrote, 'She kept on turning her head away or clamping her teeth shut.' Later Claire recorded that at lunch she said, 'I'm tired of life.'

A visit from the Practice Sister was reassuring. She gave her an enema successfully and brought more pads and some tins of a liquid complete diet. Claire recorded:

After this Grandma had a sleep. Later she tried to explain at some length what her feelings were about Mum being away. She kept saying she felt strange and peculiar. When we tried to analyse it further she said she was worried but accepted that Mum would be back soon, that it was good for Mum to have a holiday and we were all there to look after her. She was not weepy or gasping but as near as she could be to proper conversation, except that she couldn't remember the words for what she was trying to say. She drank a cup of the liquid food and ate one and a half slices of bread and jam for her tea. She accepted me very slowly feeding her, but continually said she shouldn't eat my food and shouldn't be greedy.

One night when Katherine put her to bed she brought little Clare, now six, to listen to a Bible story with Great-Grandma. She read the birth of Jesus and this delighted both the old and the young listeners. Then she thought to put a photo of me near Mother and recorded that she said, 'Is this Prue? Have I really got Prue down there?' She stroked the photo with her fingers and went to sleep happily. 'She smiled at least four times – a record!' Katherine concluded the day's entry.

The next day she was quite manageable. Helen and Gavin with 'Daniel therapy' as Helen put it, got her up and spent more time looking at old photo albums with her. Claire made her 'a kind of Spanish omelette' for lunch with vegetables and fed her two-thirds of it, followed by a baby-food semolina fruit pudding. Daniel and she were fed side by side, like two babies with a gap of eighty-six years between them!

At least they felt she had had a good meal and on the strength of it they all took her a twelve-mile drive to Allendale and sat her by the river while Helen, Gavin and little Clare swam and splashed. When it came on to rain they went to a teashop in the town which she seemed to enjoy. The main problem was getting her in and out of the car. She was losing the ability to co-operate in what is really quite a complicated manoeuvre. Unless a body bends hips, knees and neck in a co-ordinated way it can be almost impossible as I was to find out later.

This good day was interspersed with bouts of weeping and once a sort of panic attack when Katherine found her gasping for breath, leaning on the mantelpiece in her sitting-room. She clung to Katherine, crying that things were terribly, badly wrong but she didn't know how. Katherine said, 'It's probably because of Mum being away and it's perfectly natural you should feel things are wrong, but she'll be back in four days.' Mother said, 'Oh, really? That would be heaven.' As Katherine soothed her and drew a mental picture of my coming back she became quite reasonable and said she knew nothing was really wrong and they had all been kindness itself and she loved seeing 'the little baby'. She grew all warm and grateful then, a glimpse of her true personality shining through, and called Katherine 'kind and wise', following her into the bungalow kitchen to see what she could do to help, something she hadn't done for a long time. Katherine wrote, 'She flapped about with a cloth and said, "I don't know where to *find* myself" which seemed quite existential.'

One morning little Clare sat with her Great-grandma showing her photos and found one of her own mother as a baby. She said, 'Let's read the writing' and began spelling it out 'Huh-e-le-e-nuh', the way she was being taught to read at school. Mother was totally baffled and said, 'What do you mean? Huh-e-le-e-nuh?' Katherine, who was there, said how sweet but poignant it was to see a six year old trying to explain the caption to an eighty-seven year old. Little Clare was amazingly understanding with Mother. Once when Helen took her over with her for the early morning duty and was having a struggle getting Grandma dressed, Clare commented, in a sweet, comical voice, 'Yes, that dress is *appalling* to get on,' which amused Mother very much. She didn't seem to mind the little girl being there at all and sometimes showed her real affection, just like her old self. It upset her, though, if baby Daniel cried and when he didn't understand what was said to him. She thought he was being naughty and needing disciplining! Once she called him 'a vile sort of species of boy' which was most extraordinarily out of character.

Another great difficulty they had with her concerned her dentures. Mother had kept her teeth well into old age but now had one set of dentures. The Sister had managed to get them out and cleaned them on one of her visits but the girls had awful struggles and often had to leave them in though they became slimy and unpleasant. Getting them back in again, if they had succeeded in getting them out and cleaning them, was just as difficult.

On the second Sunday she seemed better and they managed to take her to church with them and though she gasped a lot and said, 'I don't need that' when offered the Communion bread, she did take it and they felt it had been quite a success. So in the afternoon they took her a drive in the country, this time in Claire's car more slowly and sedately than the way Gavin drove in our second car, and she appeared to enjoy herself. But that evening when she wouldn't eat her supper Helen said, 'Mum would want you to' and told her I would be home the day after tomorrow. She said, 'Are you sure about it?' and began crying uncontrollably.

Reading up what the family wrote in those ten days made me feel guilty about leaving her. At the time I hadn't equated her emotional state with that of a small toddler but I can see now that her reactions were very similar to those of little children deprived of their mothers. They alternate between periods of clinging affection to substitute carers, bursts of crying and tantrums and occasional carefree moments when they are distracted by amusements and treats.

On the day of our arrival she was apparently very low and wouldn't be convinced we were coming. We arrived shortly after lunch and I'll never forget the sight of her at the door, held up between tall Helen and Claire, a pale, pinched little figure, somehow bedraggled-looking because of some lunch stains down her dress and her teeth not in. She seemed more bewildered than overjoyed by our return and I think that again was very childlike. There is a deep-seated resentment against the one who has deserted you. It takes time to fall back into the old relationship, and time of course was against Mother, whose condition was deteriorating quite rapidly.

Despite my guilt feelings, however, I believe the experience was, by the grace of God, a very positive one for all the family, who have remained closely knit together in a way which is quite rare these days. And I am sure that even little Clare, young as she was, was blessed through it. She has developed into a lovely, compassionate Christian girl, now in her last year at school and with plans to read Medicine at university.

There is no pain, no sorrow, no suffering from which God cannot draw goodness – if only there is love present – and I do thank him that there was an abundance of love shown to Mother even though at times she must have felt lost and abandoned.

Family group in Prue's garden
Standing: Helen, Mark, Paul (Helen's husband) Alan
Seated: Claire, Prue with Clare (aged 7),
Mother (aged 87) with Daniel (about 8 months) and Katherine

12
Fragile as Porcelain

I tried to hold some of our holiday memories in my mind, like our camping spot on Mull when the mist suddenly blew away to show us Coll and Tiree beyond Gometra and Ulva, or the day when we drove from the midge-laden drizzle of Glen Affric to the east coast at Findochty, where the sun shone on wild waves and a gale to take our breath away yanked out the tent pegs as fast as we drove them in. We hadn't had any settled weather but we had enjoyed a great variety of scenery and were both refreshed in body, soul and spirit and most thankful to the family for letting us go.

But I was quickly engulfed again in the day-to-day caring for Mother. Only a week after our return she was suddenly unwell with a pain across her chest and extreme pallor. The doctor said she might have had a slight heart attack. She was very tired and ate almost nothing all day. Then the next day she brightened and was more smiling than she had been for a long time. In the evening she even made a joke when I was trying to get her to take her Horlicks. I said, 'You'll have to tip the cup if you want to drink it all.' 'Oh,' she said, 'they want a tip, do they?'

There was a strange little incident one day which illustrates the crisis of identity which must afflict dementia sufferers. I treated it in a matter-of-fact way at the time. I suppose I was too close to events to consider it very deeply. Now, reading it in the whole context of Mother's decline, I feel it to be startlingly illuminating.

The diary record says:

> Mother took a book out of her bookcase and
> found her name inside the front cover. She
> said, 'Agnes. That's strange. That's me. That
> was me. I don't like that. I don't know where
> that goes on. Agnes. That's peculiar. I mean –
> there's Agnes. I can't do any more about it than
> that. It looks poor.' All this was said very
> slowly with long pauses. I asked, 'What's
> peculiar about finding your name in your own
> book?' She said, 'Well, I don't know.' Then she
> picked up one of her two illustrated books
> about the royal family. 'Well, there's that,' she
> said. 'That's a very good book.' And she began
> happily to study the big coloured photos of
> people she knew she could identify even if she
> couldn't say their names.

I see now how sad it was that she didn't want to confront
her own identity. She no longer felt that she was the
person she had known as Agnes. She was relieved to
escape to the equivalent of brightly coloured toys for a
baby. And as a baby emerges from awareness of
sensations and immediate surroundings to a sense of his
own being, so Mother was retreating from her own
persona into a babylike reaction to the things around her.
The process went in fits and starts, also like a baby's
development, not in a regular downward curve, so that
some days she would seem bright and lucid and others
very vague and confused.

The diary entry for 12th August 1987 read:

> I had a battle royal to persuade her to take her
> bran so I gave up on her cup of tea and left it
> with her. It remained untouched. She thought

I was cross with her, so I said, 'Look, we can't have this. I promise I'll stop bullying you about it and just put food and drink in front of you. If you don't take it you might have to go to hospital and be put on a drip and you wouldn't like that.' She agreed vigorously. I hated seeming to threaten her but surprisingly it worked, at least this morning. I put a glass of orange juice on her table and went away and she drank it and when I filled it again she had more. Gavin helped make lunch and he and I ate ours with enjoyment. Mother read the tomato ketchup bottle instead of eating, but Gavin took our plates away and washed up and I sat beside her reading the paper and presently she began eating with her fingers and nearly cleared her plate.

Unfortunately the day ended badly. She wouldn't drink any Horlicks and she wouldn't have her teeth out to clean. I gave up, but she finds it just as unkind if I give up as if I try to force her. She takes it as a reproach to her. I resolved when I at last got her into bed that I would not have fights with her. I must not question her about why she resists things because she obviously wouldn't intentionally be troublesome. That was never her nature. I have to told on to that memory.

I tried to keep up this resolution and there were days when she did eat, especially, like a child, if I wasn't looking. The curate was now bringing her Communion at home and his visit plus a succession of relatives and friends over a few days definitely brightened her up and helped her to make an effort. But this left her very tired at night and one evening when I suggested a bath she said she was too tired. 'Ah,' I said, smiling, 'but whenever I suggest a bath you'll be tired.' She smiled and said, 'Oh, I think I've got more veracity than that.' That was a really astonishing response, showing that she understood my underlying meaning and could give an apt reply using an abstract noun in a correct context. It was one of those rare flashes of coherence which were now quite unnerving from someone who the next moment absolutely refused to go to the toilet before bed.

On 16th August 1987, a Sunday, I find an insertion by Gavin in the diary which illustrates how uninhibited Mother could be if she felt provoked and I'm afraid Gavin, with the mischief of youth, sometimes tried things out deliberately to see what she would do or say.

Gavin wrote:

> Mark went to fetch Grandma over for Sunday lunch but she wouldn't come. Eventually Mum managed to bring her. When she wouldn't eat a thing I launched into a long emotional speech about how Mum had made this lovely meal specially for her and she was rejecting it. She suddenly reared herself up and said with heavy sarcasm, 'Well, I *am* sorry for her. I hope it hasn't worn her out too much.' Mum said, 'Well, *I've* enjoyed the meal,' and we all agreed. Grandma said, 'And *I've* enjoyed it,' looking with satisfaction at her untouched food. When Dad and I said she hadn't had any of it she turned to Mark and said with great scorn, 'Wouldn't it be fine if things weren't so stupid? So many things are said.' Later she suddenly said, looking at her food, 'I wonder if one could sell it.' A minute later she told Mum, 'I'm not rejecting your cooking.' I said, 'But you were going to sell it.' She exclaimed with great

energy, 'I've never heard such donkey things.' She actually ended by telling me to 'Shut up please.'

We had to laugh about it. It wasn't the way I handled Mother but at least it had stimulated her to carry in her memory for a few minutes the theme of rejecting food, but as she didn't eat it in the end there was no satisfactory outcome.

Two days later I had a visitor from our Newcastle days to lunch and tea. Mother didn't recognise her and kept saying, 'That lady's looking at me.' She ate a tiny portion of the sweet at lunch but nothing else. At tea there was ham and salad, home-made bread and butter, a cream cake and chocolate mousse. Mother said, 'I don't know what I'm to do. I don't see anything to eat.' Whatever I put on her plate she said, 'Yes, well I don't want that' or 'That's no good.' She was very miserable.

After the visitor had gone Mother wouldn't co-operate with undressing though she was exhausted. She kept repeating, 'I wish you'd help me, I thought you'd help me.' She began crying at the thought of how tired she was. I got her to bed at last but she went on crying, saying things like, 'Is it worth it?'

It was the first time I longed for death to release her from this misery. The diary entry says:

> I couldn't help kneeling at her bedside and praying for her to slip quietly away to find peace. I said all I could think of aloud to her: 'Darling, you are surrounded by love: the love of God and the love of your daughter.' I spoke of the everlasting arms. I think her distress began to change into tears of sorrow at her own restlessness and she half-admitted they were

tears of joy but I didn't feel she was satisfied and relaxed as she usually is when she sinks down on her pillow. I knelt by the bed for some while holding her hand.

These were the first signs that the time would come when real love would not appear to make any difference to her and this was the hardest lesson to learn – to keep on loving in the face of apparent rejection.

The physical caring caused both her and me enough distress in itself. There was more trouble over her constipation and even the sweet Practice Sister and I couldn't get her to co-operate for an enema. I wrote in the diary:

> Mother expressed astonishment that I would let her be treated like this. When at length we managed to administer the enema she fought both of us over going to the toilet. She now has a commode in her room and we finally managed to push her on after chasing her round the room with it. We tried to laugh but it wasn't funny at all. At least Sister saw her at her worst and realised what it's like for me on my own with her. She agreed to come three times a week to see if we can keep her regular to help her appetite too.

On 20th August 1987 I noted:

> Sister surprised me by saying that if she got old and confused she'd like to be like Mother – totally without memory or understanding of how confused she is. But Mother can be both miserable and frightened, saying things like 'Life is so strange' or 'Things are so different'

which suggest some awareness and she sits moaning, 'Oh oh oh' for long periods of time.

There were days when I longed for intellectual stimulus – to share with Gavin his reading of Shaw and Ibsen which he was studying to prepare for the English degree he would commence at Durham in the autumn. The diary doesn't even mention my delight when his A Level results came and he had three A's. I suppose I told Mother but I don't think it made much impact on her.

It was the physical things that made the impact these days and I began to realise that trying to push food into her mouth was a bodily assault just as bad as trying to press her onto the toilet or lift her legs into the bath or out again. I wrote on 23rd August 1987:

> All such things are an attack on her person, a sort of violation to which she is acutely sensitive, just as she's sensitive to the slightest bump or knock or sudden movement or loud sound. She goes around in a sort of porcelain condition – very fragile. She is afraid to step off steps or walk on rough ground.

Despite this, I still took her out for walks and she was always better for the exercise and the increased flow of oxygen to the brain. Sometimes too the stimulus of other faces helped, especially children. Helen brought her two over before the end of the school holidays. I recorded the day in these words:

> Though Mother spoke of Daniel as naughty when he crawled about, banging toys on our living-room floor, she was actually uplifted by the whole day. Little Clare was extremely good and loving and for the last hour Mother thought Daniel sweet and quiet and adorable.

I knew she was susceptible to noise so I wasn't surprised when that upset her but I don't think I'd realised how delicately balanced her emotions were. When I took her over to her bungalow after they'd gone she was almost weeping not with the usual misery but with a kind of loving elation. I wrote:

> She seized my hand, kissed it, said her home was 'beautiful' and spoke of how God had blessed her. Toilet was still going to be a difficulty because she said, 'We can't have that after . . .' but a very gentle cajoling sufficed to get her on. Similarly with her teeth. I guided her own hand to them and she took them out herself saying, 'The Lord would want me to do that.' She seemed much more peaceful and gentle and amenable when I got her to bed. What an amazing difference!

I can only think that the presence of the children and especially the spontaneous love shown her by little Clare refreshed her spirit just as walking out in the air refreshed her body. The next time the Sister called she thought her much better and on 30th August, after much prayer, we took her to church with us and all went well.

I'm sure these small times of improvement were sent by God. The joy they brought was intense, a pure spiritual joy, which we would never perhaps have experienced without the trials in between. They showed us too that Mother was really there, beyond the dementia, and gave a spur to our love which so often seemed to us – in our human frailty – to be foundering on rocky shores.

13
Split Personality

In early September I began to notice more strongly what the family had already commented on when we were away, that Mother was often bright first thing in the morning while she was still in bed, but as soon as anything had to be done to her the gloom returned.

One day I found the hot tap full on in the bathroom so she had obviously been up but was back in bed oblivious of the running water. She seemed quite serene and commented on the bright light of the dawn when I opened the curtains. I gave her a cuddle and said, 'I do love my Mammy.' She said with just her old twinkle, 'Well, I don't know that there's much to love.' She volunteered to get up and was cheerful till the moment I started to wash her because she was a little dirty. Then the veil of misery descended again.

I talked about this to Alan and he suggested the explanation, which I am sure was right. Every time she woke refreshed from sleep she forgot her condition, but as soon as it was brought home to her again by the tasks that had to be done for her she was plunged into depression. Alone, too, she was not aware of being unable to communicate properly. But when required to speak she was increasingly unable to finish sentences. How frustrating this was for her at this stage it is difficult to guess.

It was frustrating for me when I really wanted to find something out. I had been to the market one morning and on my return to her bungalow I found her sitting brightly on her hall seat. She looked at me and said, 'Is this the lady who was here just now?' I laughed and said, 'I've just come. Was somebody here?' She said, 'I don't know. There was somebody here in a manner of speaking.' Then she pointed to the sitting-room door which was closed. 'They opened that.' I asked, 'Were there two people here?' She said, 'Oh, I wouldn't say that.' I asked if anyone had rung the bell. Had she opened the door and found someone on the doorstep? She smiled and said, 'You might think that, I suppose.' I never did find out if a visitor had called.

In contrast to this cheerful vagueness she showed flashes of violent anger from time to time, like beating her hands on the basin when I tried to wash them. I found the verbal reproaches harder to take and on 12th September 1987 I wrote in the diary:

> She was happy today as long as she lay in bed but as usual the protest began as soon as I took her to the bathroom. 'Prue, please, I've never heard of such a thing before.' When I began to put her corset on she cried, 'I'm amazed at you.' And she went on being amazed when I tried to pull on her stockings all warm from the radiator which she usually finds very comforting. She said, 'You are the most extraordinary woman. I used to love you.' Stupidly I let tears come into my eyes. I don't think I was so much hurt for myself because I knew it was the dementia speaking, but I just grieved that she could come to this, wondering what she would have thought if she'd known a year or two ago that she would ever say such a thing to me. She went rather bewildered when

she became aware of my tears, but not exactly subdued, though she did stand up when I asked her to and said, 'I'll do what I can.' I left her when she was dressed, to prepare her cereal, and I was calm and cheerful again when I brought her into the kitchen for her breakfast. She was still rather rebellious, pushing her chair back with her legs when I tried to get her to sit, but at last I managed it. Then she pushed the bowl away several times. I put the spoon into her hands and told her how good she'd been lately, feeding herself. At last I left her to go and hang my own washing out and have some breakfast myself and write this. It's a relief writing it, and if this is a new phase – there have been signs before, of course – of abuse and temper, then I think with God's help I can cope and not get upset. 'Do good to them that despitefully use you.' Simple obedience to that precept – in the knowledge that she doesn't mean it – is the only way.

I remember too that I clung to the word 'If you do it unto one of the least of these my brethren you do it unto me.' Because Mother was like a different creature from the Mother I had known all my life it helped to keep reminding myself, 'You are doing this for Jesus.' I still tried to draw her into family things as I always had but she would become this strange alien being all in a moment.

It was Mark's twenty-fourth birthday on 16th September and as he was always keen on cycling I had bought him a comic card of an elephant riding on a penny-farthing. I showed it to Mother, but when I tried to take it back to write in she clung on tight to it with both hands and began kissing the picture, grinning and making clucking noises. Just for a few moments she looked like a real caricature of a mad woman in Bedlam.

The doctor was now aware that I needed more relief and she telephoned to say that a social worker would come to discuss Dene Park, the local authority home, for possible day care once a week or for respite care for holidays. A raised seat for the toilet was fixed and also one for the bath. The toilet one certainly made it easier to sit Mother down but didn't, of course, eliminate the problem of her refusing to go anywhere near it. The bath seat might have helped if I could have persuaded her to sit on it and swing her legs over but this she absolutely would not do. Two home helps were also to come for occasional relief when I wanted to go out, one actually to put her bed on the monthly dinner-and-talk evenings. I couldn't imagine how a stranger would achieve this but Mother behaved much better with her and on her second visit said, 'Oh, to see your beautiful face!' Looking back I realise that this was the first definite evidence I had that a full-time Home for her might be the kindest thing but at that point I hadn't begun to consider the possibility.

At the beginning of October I received some information about the Alzheimer's Society and two pieces of advice in the booklet were particularly helpful: 1. Avoid confrontation by going along with the confusion gently and distracting attention where possible; 2. Remember that dementia sufferers may not understand what you are saying to them.

The advice was common sense, of course, and I had thought on the same lines myself over the months but seeing it written down like that focused my mind wonderfully on the pointlessness of arguments and efforts to reason with Mother. I became more peaceful in my dealings with her even though she herself was not noticeably more content.

However, the flashes of temper did seem to decrease though there was one, surprisingly, during *Songs of Praise*. She was supposed to be eating her tea but had messed her bread around for an hour and a half. She didn't want me to leave for Evensong so I stayed, knitting and listening to the programme. Suddenly she banged her arms around and exclaimed, 'Why don't you – ?' and then she stopped as suddenly. I laid down my knitting and went and sat beside her and she was instantly contrite. 'I'm sorry, I'm sorry. I don't know why – .' At last she ate a few pieces of bread and later went to bed 'normally'.

Again it was purely childlike attention seeking, I suppose. Perhaps she wanted me to take notice that she wasn't eating her tea. So, even with all the advice and help I was now getting, it was still hard to be sure what was the best way to handle her in her different moods.

When I turned to prayer and reading the Bible, especially the Sermon on the Mount, I always experienced a calming of the spirit, but I know that I didn't wait often enough upon God in the trying moments throughout the day: the endless 'accidents' when she had just been changed into clean clothes, the carefully prepared food messed about but uneaten. The temptation was to act first in my own strength which then often failed pathetically, rather than to look upwards for help before turning thought into speech or action. All the time it was a learning experience and, in looking back and reliving it and meditating on how I might have done better, I am still learning.

14
Moments of Joy, Moments of Sadness

On 4th October 1987 we took Gavin to Durham for the beginning of his university life. Thanks to Helen, Claire and Katherine who all came with little Clare too, Alan and I were both able to go and share this new experience with him. I didn't bring Mother to lunch with us all because it was a pouring wet day, but the others all went over to her bungalow afterwards to be with her till we got back. Mother was delighted, as always, to see little Clare.

We installed Gavin in his college room with a cheery sounding room-mate. He looked a little wan when we left but we knew he would enter into his new life with zest. Now, with Alan out all day and no sons to feed at lunchtime I had more time to deal with Mother and she was certainly becoming a full-time job.

As autumn closed in her moods swung more than ever. One day she started off calling me 'lovely and sweet and funny' while she was still in bed but as I began to dress her, smiling encouragingly, she snapped, 'What are you smiling for?' Then a few moments later muttered under her breath, 'I hate you.' At once she asked, 'What did you say?' as if I'd said it. Maybe she thought I had. I said, 'What did *you* say?' She said, 'I don't know. Something nice, I hope.' I knew that one of her frequent expressions when being toileted, bathed or dressed was 'I hate this kind of life.' So she was only transferring her feeling to the one doing it all to her. This time a swift prayer for God's love to surround us both stopped me from feeling hurt. I took her into her sitting-room and read her morning psalm to her and left her with her breakfast. She was brighter later and even survived a visit to the toilet without too much moaning, though she said when I pulled her knickers up, 'Nobody else has this sort of thing.' I said laughing, 'All women wear knickers – even the Queen.' 'Oh, surely not?' she said, really astonished.

Though I was round at her bungalow by seven o'clock in the morning there was sometimes evidence that she had been up already. One day a vase of flowers in her sitting-room had been knocked over. Another time the little cotton chair arms that she fiddled with all the time were in bed with her. Often she had had accidents which had to be cleaned up but she watched without interest as if they were nothing to do with her.

But on 16th October 1987 there was quite a different scenario. She was all aglow and desperate to tell me something. 'It was very interesting . . . I really enjoyed it . . . it was quite extraordinary . . . I'll tell you because you would be interested.' All this with long pauses and even during a visit to the toilet. I asked her if it was a dream. 'Yes, it would be . . . well, no . . . it wasn't a dream.' I gave her a cup of tea. 'Yes, this is what I wanted . . . but I couldn't go there in my shoes.' I remembered that she had been walking about the room when I came in with one bedsock off and the other in her hand. She kept saying she would tell me. 'It was wonderful . . . well, we had a very small part, a very good . . . really it absolutely was . . .' She seemed so happy that I asked, 'Was it spiritual?' She said, 'I'd be pleased to think it was. It was beautiful in many ways . . . I think if I was to . . . what is it . . . yes . . . almost . . .' I do believe she had had in her inmost soul, which was beyond the dementia, a glimpse of heaven either in a vision or dream, but to bring it out through her poor denuded brain and powers of speech was impossible.

Alas, it had faded by the evening. When I took her teeth out – a little quickly to catch her unawares before she fought it – she said, 'How could you? That was a dastardly thing to do.' She could certainly find words when she was angry!

Not long afterwards we had one of those benign autumn days, very still, when the trees, in red and gold and bronze, basked in the valley aglow with sunshine. I was determined to get her into the car and take her out to enjoy it. At first she wasn't very responsive even when I'd got her to take a little walk from the car and look at the colourful panorama. But I found some blackberries and began picking and after about five minutes she said, 'I did this with Janet.' I was delighted that this old memory had resurfaced and that she had found the words to express it.

But it was only the next day that I recorded the first time she was really aggressive, not just resistant. I suppose I was exasperated to start with because she had eaten hardly any tea and had refused her Complan as well. When I took her to the bathroom I pulled her sleeves up for a wash. She pulled them down at once and I pulled them up again without comment. At once she raised her fist as though to hit me and her face was distorted with rage. The look went as quickly as it had come, as if her real self had seen my dismayed face and taken over again. 'How desperately near the surface evil and violence are in all of us,' I wrote in the diary afterwards. 'I hugged her and kissed her with tears in my eyes. She went all soft and sad and said she'd do anything to please me, so I said, "Will you drink your Horlicks, then?" and she did, most of it, quite quickly. This could all have been avoided if I hadn't employed deliberate confrontation – just what I know I must avoid.'

The next day another first happened. She tried to say my name and couldn't. The diary says:

> I greeted her with 'Hello, darling Mammy,' in the funny voice she likes. She said, 'Hello, darling – Helen?' I said, 'You've forgotten my name?' She said, 'Yes,' quite openly. 'Prue,' I said. 'Oh yes, darling Prue.'

Yet another first a few days later: an absolute refusal to get up off the settee at bedtime. This was to prove a great trouble almost every night from then on. I tried the usual persuasions – 'Do it for my sake'; 'You do want to please me?' and even 'This is what the Lord wants you to do.' I wondered if I would have to get Alan to lift her but I was reluctant to use force. I went out of the room for a moment and prayed, 'Please help, Lord.' Just realising he knew all about it was a joyful feeling. I went back and held out my arms in front of her. She said, 'I want to do what's . . .' I said, 'Come along then, my pet,' and at last she came, but she was very wretched. I'm sure now that it was dread of all the washing and dressing processes that produced the reluctance to get up in the morning and the new resistance to going to bed.

But there were comical little signs of self-awareness still. The next time she lifted her fists in anger she dropped them suddenly and said, 'No, I don't do that, do I?' I said, 'No, you don't. That's not you.'

I tried often to make her laugh but it was getting much harder. On 23rd October we had another beautiful autumn day. The diary entry reads:

I put her into her coat, gloves, hat and scarf after lunch and let her sit on the seat on her south-facing patio while I tided up her garden and swept the paths, keeping in sight of her all the time. She actually called out, 'What can I do to help?' I couldn't think of anything and she didn't repeat it but it was a change and showed she was feeling lively. So I suggested a walk and she came gladly. As we approached the hill in front of our house she said, 'Poor old lady going down the hill.' I said, 'Poor old lady has to come back up which is worse,' and she almost laughed. I said, 'You laughed. You really did.' She said, 'I don't think I'd have done a thing like that,' laughing some more.

On our return she protested but in a good-humoured way when I removed her outdoor things, so I stuck her hat flat on top of my head and she laughed outright. We had a cup of tea to warm us up but she didn't start hers. I said, 'Drink your tea. It's lovely.' She clasped the cup with her hands and said it was too hot. 'Try the handle,' I suggested but she didn't seem able to find it. I said, 'Well now, how are we going to get that nice tea down inside you?' And she said with a little laugh, 'I don't know. I can't see it ever happening.'

Moments of happy banter like this were rare but they helped me to feel that the Mother I knew was still with me. I needed her companionship in the long days alone with her, yet for so many sad hours the being who was there was a lost, unrecognisable soul.

No part of my experience of caring over the years – in teaching, in the upbringing of children, in work I did with young delinquents on Community Service, even in eight years of looking after old people when Alan's mother and stepfather lived with us till their deaths – none of this was like caring for someone with dementia. I was feeling my way in the minute by minute interaction with a changed mother, and in learning and applying my lesson of love I was still a stumbling novice.

15
I Receive More Help

At the end of October a gentleman from Social Services arrived with a frame to go round the toilet. Mother liked to have things to hold on to because of her loss of a sense of security. I had long since removed the towel rail from the wall opposite. She would cling to it with great force to prevent me from easing her towards the toilet seat. I hoped the frame would give her more confidence to sit down.

The man said, 'I'll send a builder to fasten it down.' I said, 'It's perfectly simple – just three screws in each foot. I can do it.' He said, 'Oh I know, but then we'd have a problem if there was any claim against the authority and our man hadn't done it.' As he was going out he said, 'She can use it now but if she puts weight right at the front it'll tip over till it's fastened down.' The illogicality of this didn't seem to strike him at all.

In fact that night Mother wouldn't touch the handles of the frame but clung on to the bathroom shelf. She was in her most obstinate mood and I couldn't get her to take her teeth out either. Eventually I had to hold her hand by main force and winkle them out with my other hand. She saw I was at my wit's end and kept saying, 'Just tell me what to do,' which was even more aggravating.

It's easy to see with hindsight that I was becoming worn down. Of course, greater closeness to God would have alleviated this but I dare not assert that it could have prevented it altogether. Our Lord became exhausted when the crowds pressed upon him relentlessly and no one was closer to the Father than he. I know that I should have spent more time just absorbing God's love by waiting upon him in silence in the brief interludes I had, but I might still have come to the end of my nervous energy because of the hourly struggle to help someone who could no longer co-operate, in fact who was actively and fiercely resistant.

Fortunately I was given the chance of a day out soon after this when two of the Crossroads ladies came between 10.30 and 3.45 on the day before my birthday and I met Katherine in Newcastle for some shopping. Katherine had the good idea of getting a book with lots of pictures of babies in and putting some round the bungalow. We came back together as she was going to stay over the weekend of my birthday, and Mother was pleased to see us and was very responsive to the baby photographs.

The home help who was coming once a month to put her to bed had now made her second visit and I asked her how she'd managed. She said, 'The teeth were easy but the toilet was trickier.' But it was evident that Mother was more submissive to a stranger. I stored this up in my mind but had no thought of acting upon it at that stage. Still, it was an amazing feeling for me to come back from an evening out and know I could go straight to bed because Mother was already tucked up asleep!

Sometimes Alan came and watched television in Mother's bungalow so we could be together and occasionally he could cajole her into getting up off the settee at bedtime but she would have been terribly upset if I'd asked him to help undress her.

The Practice Sister, who called regularly, was now getting concerned that I needed a break, though I felt my health was as good as ever. She told us about a small private Home which a nurse friend of hers had recently started. I hope I prayed about it but the Diary doesn't say. I know I took some persuading and eventually said, 'Maybe Mother could try a weekend there.' She thought it ought to be a week at least but I didn't feel either Mother or I was ready for that. So Alan and I went to look at the place, which was quarter of an hour's walk away, and arranged for her to go the weekend after her eighty-eighth birthday. It was a pleasant old house set amid trees and the proprietor and her husband were a most caring and loving couple, living in a flat with their two children at the top of the house. I had no fears about how well Mother would be cared for but I did wonder very much how she would react and if the Home really understood what they were taking on.

She was particularly difficult on the Thursday before she was to go. There were days when I succeeded with her because I felt truly full of love and then there were days when I just didn't measure up and found myself having to push and pull her to get anywhere at all. I know I was never rough but I hated to feel her resistance and I knew how near I sometimes was to stepping over the borderline to violence. Somehow, by the grace of God, I never did but it has made me very wary of condemning people who do lose their tempers with really recalcitrant patients.

I wrote in my diary:

> Anyone in Mother's condition can only be loved by an utterly pure, disinterested love. It is the pearl of great price, hidden by our Lord in his field. I have had it in my grasp a few times but I always let it slip. When I have it Mother has sometimes said, 'How kind you

are!' but that true love has to be above needing any reward, lovely as such a response is. If I could only get it in my grasp again and not let go! Am I giving in by sending her to South Park for two days? Perhaps I'll get a little nervous strength back. Perhaps she will gain something herself. Whatever the result we should be happier to see each other on Monday morning.

I now believe that God put this little respite in my way at just the right moment and I had no need to feel doubts about it. But I was anxious and tried to prepare Mother by saying she was to have a little holiday, although I hadn't much hope that she was taking it in.

It was only for two days but I knew in my heart of hearts that it might be the start of a bigger move and I had very mixed feelings of guilt and relief, apprehension and hope when the morning of 14th November 1987 dawned.

The diary entry for that day begins:

Mother's first words this morning were, 'I'm not going *there*.' I was horrified. How could she have remembered about the Home? And if she had was she so set against it that I might not be able to get her there? But as soon as I turned back the covers I realised it wasn't South Park at all but her old enemy, the toilet. She had soiled her pad in the night. I was so relieved about that that I soon cleaned her up, despite the usual protests and kept telling her very cheerfully that today was the day her little holiday started.

She made no response to that but I managed to feed her some breakfast and about ten o'clock Alan and I had a big struggle to get her into the car. It wasn't because she understood what was happening. The manoeuvre was just becoming harder and harder for her to accomplish and getting out at the end of the short journey was even worse. So she was quite upset by the time we entered South Park House. Mrs Watson, the proprietor, was there to greet her, however, and took her hand and said she'd make her a nice cup of tea. Mother instantly put on her best party manners and was really profuse: 'How kind you are!'

We were encouraged to leave fairly quickly as one is with small children on their first day at school and we didn't visit again that day so that she would have a chance to bond with Mrs Watson and the friendly staff. A telephone call established that all was well and she had eaten splendidly!

We went to see her on the Sunday morning after church and found her in the lounge with a lady who had recognised her from meeting her at the hairdresser's. The lady knew me too when I came in but Mother said, 'This is my daughter,' actually trying to effect a proper introduction, though she couldn't say the lady's name. This was a delightful surprise. She knew Alan too when he came close though when he sat further off she said, 'Who is that nice man?' I told her it was Alan and she said, 'I thought it was.'

Presently the other ladies in the lounge wanted to go to their rooms to watch the Sunday service on television, so we took Mother to hers. There was no television in the lounge. This was to encourage conversation and prevent arguments over programmes, which seemed a sensible idea. Mother was less wild-eyed than she had been of late though rather vague and bewildered when we settled her to watch the service herself. I said, 'See you in the morning' and she replied, 'That'll never come' but there were no tears.

On Monday morning I went alone to fetch Mother as Alan was back at work. I found her with her breakfast tray still in front of her. Her cereal was eaten but there was still some toast so they were doing what I had suggested, leaving it to see if she would finish it. One of the staff went to fetch her medicines and Mother said, 'I don't want to say anything about anybody but . . .' I guessed she had vague memories of toilet and washing problems, so I said, 'I'm sure everyone's been very kind.'

When the girl came back she described how Mother had been chatting to everyone in the lounge and really held a conversation. I said to Mother, 'It sounds as if you've had a very good time.' She said, 'Well, I made an effort.'

In the diary that evening I commented:

> This seems to be the crux of the matter. She did make an effort. With me she doesn't. Several times during the day she has said, 'You will be kind to me, won't you?' which makes me wonder how well she remembers all the wretched battles we have had. She did seem pleased to see me this morning all the same.

When Mrs Stobbart came that week she thought Mother seemed brighter and she ate all her dinner without trouble. I had taken her a walk every day it was fine and though it was often a struggle to get her over the doorstep she managed about half a mile each time. The weekend break was definitely a stimulus and with improved eating her vigour returned and the confusion seemed a little less.

Even so it was during that week that I came in to hear her say, 'Who is it?' and when I stood in front of her, smiling and saying, 'Hello, my pet,' she stared hard at me and said, 'Who are you?' Later she was quite jolly and I put on the television and found a snooker tournament. 'That's snooker,' I said, 'what you call billiards.' 'Billions,' she said. 'No, billiards.' She gave quite a laugh and said, 'If I want to call it billions, I will.' I soon forgot about her not knowing me but when I look back at the diary I realise that was the first sign of a new phase. I don't think she was blotting me out because I had sent her away for the weekend but perhaps she just couldn't cope with two different realities.

I did thank God that she had seemed to be brighter at South Park than she was at home, certainly as bright as she was capable of being at that stage, but any recollection of it was gone within a day or two.

Unfortunately the next time the Sister came to give her a bath and hairwash Mother was the worst she had ever been. She fought her, kicking her leg and actually slapping her with her hand. Struggling to help I kept saying I was so ashamed of her behaviour, just as if she had been a naughty child, but Sister was very sweet and gave her a cuddle before she went and said she hoped they were still friends.

It was that very same afternoon that Katherine came with her boyfriend, Michael, and they announced their engagement. It wasn't unexpected but I was full of joy and ran over to bring Mother to join us for tea. I told her the news as we walked over and she gave Katherine a big hug as soon as she was in the house and Michael a kiss. She seemed to understand, although at tea she asked at least four times who Michael was. Her occasional remarks, though, were happy, if a little bewildered: 'It's so beautiful. Why is it so beautiful?' Once she said, 'The children have such lovely hair,' looking at them as they sat opposite to her, quite radiant.

She was very frightened about being walked back in the dark afterwards to her bungalow but for once I got her into bed without tears. There was no doubt that she could pick up on an atmosphere of happiness which makes me wonder again how far a really joyful presence all the time would have held at bay the misery into which she so often sank.

At South Park, with plenty of people around, there was a general air of cheerfulness and she had just enough of her old social sense left to make her feel obliged to respond. At home, though she still had visitors, her company was limited to me and I had to leave her alone for short periods in the day and at night. If only I had been more full of the fruit of the Holy Spirit, especially the first two qualities of love and joy, I'm sure I could have helped her more than I did. What poignancy there is in 'if only'!

16

A Harrowing Dilemma

During the remaining weeks of 1987 there was a noticeable reduction in Mother's ability to say whole sentences. She could manage short ones like 'You will be kind' or 'I'm so frightened' and once when I walked her over for Sunday lunch and she was panicking as usual at coming outside she said, 'I'm too small.' But most conversations deteriorated into 'Why did I - ?'; 'If you could just let me - ?' and any effort on my part to find out what she was trying to say just made her more upset.

On 6th December she had a visit which stimulated her into an extra effort. Mark came with his girlfriend, Phyllis, and I let him take her over to see Mother and then followed when I thought they had probably stayed long enough. Mark told me that Grandma had said little but as they were leaving she managed to say, 'I'm sorry to see the end of you' which, if a little oddly phrased, made sense in the context. Fortunately Phyllis was most understanding and sympathetic. As a trained psychologist with plenty of work experience she quickly sized Mother up and realised what stage she had reached, so that nothing in her manner surprised or bothered her.

The doctor came to give Mother a check-up soon after that and said that her pulse was strong and steady and she was in good physical health. As she was going she said to Mother, 'I'll leave you in peace.' Mother said, 'In pieces more like,' which surprised us both. I just wished she had laughed when she said it to show that her sense of humour was still active. The doctor advised me not to worry about her teeth as her diet was so soft now. So she wore them for only about five hours during the next fortnight. The Sister managed to insert them at her next visit but that night the Home Help came to put Mother to bed and proudly left a note saying, 'Managed teeth and toilet this time.' I didn't get them in again for quite a while.

We tried another weekend at South Park a month after the first. She was less responsive but when I went to fetch her she burst into tears at the sight of me. Even so she managed to say to the staff as I took her out, 'You've been very good,' which showed that her old sweet manner could still rise to the surface on occasions.

For a while afterwards she was clingy and affectionate like a child restored to its mother but the old misery took over at bedtime. I said, 'You were more serene at South Park. I thought you'd be happy to be home but you don't sound like it.' She said, 'Oh, you wouldn't do that, would you?' In the diary I made no comment on that remark, but was it possible, I ask myself now, that she sensed I might be contemplating sending her there permanently? I hardly think she was able to work out a sequence of thoughts like that but the deteriorating brain is a strange thing. Connections that one thinks have long gone suddenly spring into life again.

For long stretches of time now she would sit moaning, 'Oh oh oh' and 'Lord, have mercy' but she could still make remarks to people who called. One day she had the curate to bring her Communion and later the chiropodist to cut her toenails. With both she was co-operative and even pleasant. I know I shouldn't have found this hard to take but I'm afraid I did. Of course, I was delighted to see the misery stop for a while but I longed for her old cheerfulness when she and I were alone together.

On 17th December 1987 I wrote in the diary:

> I thought I'd got my impatience beaten but last night I pulled her hand off the shelf in the bathroom when it went back twice. She can't reach the toilet when she holds it and I was desperate to get her on to save a mess. Mrs Watson asked me – when I collected Mother last time – how I manage to toilet her alone. They always have two members of staff to take her at South Park. I admitted it was difficult but no one really knows how ghastly it is when she does everything possible to resist.

As I wrote that morning at Mother's kitchen table I could hear her in the sitting-room moaning, 'Oh oh oh' so I knew she wasn't eating. I went in to try and feed her but she just tipped her porridge off the spoon. I went back and wrote:

> She must sense I'm irritated – I'm really crying inside all the time and quite a bit outside right now. I know it's self-indulgence and lack of prayer. The family would say, 'Of course you get wild, it would send most people potty,' but I know that's not the point. Each time she's been to South Park I've had a relapse into impatience afterwards, I suppose because I've tasted the amazing freedom. I know I'm just letting irritation get hold of me, instead of love. Oh, so easy to do! But it is I who am distancing myself from God, not the other way round.

Now it saddens me to think that I was sitting apart from her when I should have been beside her. The fact was that the sight of her uneaten food was a reproach to me. If they could feed her at South Park, why couldn't I? I did realise, I think, that she was like a small child, behaving much better at nursery than she did at home, but I was also well aware that I wasn't drawing daily on that wonderful fountain of love which God pours out for all to drink at if they will. I was taking the occasional sip but I needed to empty myself first of all the frustration and irritability which prevented me from taking a full and sustaining draught.

Christmas Day came and I wrote:

> I wouldn't have believed six months ago that I would feel it right to keep her in her bungalow for Christmas. Too many people and too much noise would have overwhelmed her now. The family visited her in ones and twos. She was very happy to see little Clare and Daniel but she didn't understand about the presents they brought. Everyone was very conscious of the change in her.

Three days later the diary records:

> Tonight she was very angry when I tried to wash her and actually bit at the flannel in my hands. Our eyes met and she went quiet and said, 'I'm sorry. I didn't mean to do that.' I said, 'I know, darling, but I do sometimes wonder if I'm the right person to be looking after you. You didn't go on like this at South Park.' But she didn't know what I meant by South Park. Would she be happier there? Or if she can't be happy, would she be quieter, more apathetic? With me she seems to live on a too highly emotional level. I hope more spiritual too. She doesn't have our evening prayers

there, although one of the staff agreed to read a Bible chapter at night, which was very kind. I really am in a dilemma. I pray that I'll know when God is telling me she should be in a Home full-time. Would it save her from the anger she lets loose on me or am I deceiving myself for my own sake?

I wonder now if, unconsciously, she was reminded by my presence and her familiar surroundings how far she had moved from her true self and from our proper relationship, and this was more distressing to her bewildered mind than a neutral place and smiling unknown faces. At the time I was too close to it all to think this through.

On the last night of 1987 I begged her to be serene, even joyful. She gave no response and I came away sad. At our house Gavin, who was home for Christmas, had his new girlfriend from university staying for New Year. She was a lovely Christian girl and as I came into the kitchen where they were sitting she saw that my eyes were full of tears and she got up and put her arms round me and hugged me. Gavin was just as affectionate and their warmth and love comforted me greatly.

17
A Door Opens

At the beginning of 1988 the food and drink problem became worse. I was giving Mother all the concentrated liquid foods I could think of, trying various flavours to see what she would take, but there was little consistency in her tastes. Occasionally I tried the ploy of 'You don't want to live, do you?' which sometimes made her take some mouthfuls and then I would wonder, but why *would* anyone want to live like this?

At her first Communion in the new year she was really confused, though she did manage to join in the Lord's Prayer. But there were many 'oh oh's' during the short service. The curate was kind and wise and let nothing disturb him at all. I was glad, though, that she didn't bite his finger when he popped the wafer into her mouth. She had bitten mine that morning when I was giving her the tablet which was to prevent fluid retention. That was another struggle – to get it down her every day – but if I didn't her ankles swelled and as she would no longer consent to lie on the settee with her feet up this was yet another anxiety.

A new irritation was that she tended to cling on to cups or plates while still refusing to eat. Sometimes I had to prise one from her grip when she had sat clutching it for an hour or more. I felt cruel doing this and I know I was annoyed with her. It was so frustrating that she would neither eat nor drink and yet pretend she wanted it. 'Lord, forgive me,' I wrote in the diary on 9th January.

'Have I forgotten already that what I do for her I am doing for you?' And then I added, bitterly I fear, 'But you wouldn't fight me, would you, Lord?' I knew at the time it was a foolish thought because it was the dementia fighting me, not Mother. Perhaps I didn't wait for the Lord to answer my thought. I was always more ready to tell him my needs than I was to listen to him. I forgot that he knew my needs before I asked him and that he only wanted me to rest quietly in his love. In this drawn-out period of suffering I kept forgetting the very lessons I was trying daily to learn.

As Mother was now refusing her Horlicks at night I worried that she wouldn't sleep because she had had so little nourishment. However, on 11th January she slept till 11.30 in the morning. I kept going over to see if she was awake and her face was parchment-coloured and pinched, looking like death, with her head drooped to one side, yet her breathing was soft and regular. It seemed a pity that she had to wake to the turmoil of life, but she did eventually.

The Sister had persuaded me to let her go to South Park for a week and I told Mother very brightly that she was going to have another little holiday soon and she'd like that, wouldn't she? She made a funny face and said, 'No.' I said, 'Why d'you say that?' She said, 'Because I think no,' which was the most continuous conversation we'd had for a while. I couldn't tell whether she understood my meaning and this was a serious negative reaction or whether the words had just come out like that and she didn't know what I was talking about anyway.

She was particularly difficult at night two days before she was to go and I told her straight out that she was going to South Park for a week so that *I* could have a rest. She made no response, but next day she did seem to be trying hard to be 'good' and kept saying, 'You *are* a sweet thing,' and 'You *are* kind, aren't you?' And that night she joined in 'Our Father' with me in a loud voice. It seemed unbelievable that she could be capable of a kind of emotional blackmail when she was so far gone in dementia and yet I couldn't help wondering.

Actually the week was a success. I asked the staff for details of how they managed her and they described the complete regime, which sounded to my ears so trouble-free. They even got her to walk downstairs with one helper beside her and another going backwards ahead of her to give her confidence. She had sat in the lounge and actually initiated conversation with another lady who was confused. Mother asked, 'Can I help you?' and then said to the staff, 'Is she all right?' I was amazed and delighted to hear this. It was so much in keeping with her true character to be concerned for others. Even when she was over eighty she had been one of a team in her Newcastle parish who served coffee every week at an old people's home and she had often ministered to people many years younger than herself.

On my daily visits to South Park I saw that she was eating well, but she seemed to become more emotional while I was there, often ending up quite weepy which saddened me. One bright day I took her out for a little walk and tried to get her to look at the view from the road, pointing out the Abbey glowing in the sunshine. She glanced up, said, 'I saw it,' and looked down again at her feet. As usual she was nervous and lacking in confidence about walking outside.

I got the impression that she was unwilling to be drawn out of the daily routine there and when I told her I would be taking her home next day she said, 'That's too soon.'

Was this a true reaction or did she mean, 'Not soon enough'? It was impossible to be sure.

Shortly after she was home the social worker, who had been visiting to assess her needs, organised a case conference. She invited a specialist in the care of the elderly, the home help organiser, the head of Crossroads and a representative from Dene Park, the council home which could offer day care. The purpose was to work out a package of care which would give me some time off nearly every day! Social Services don't always get a good press but I must testify that they couldn't have been kinder or more sensitive.

Dene Park suggested day care on a Sunday and asked me to take Mother there first so that they could show her round and the carer allocated to her could chat to her. The day I took her I simply could not get her out of the car when we reached the place and two helpers had to come out; finally we all three succeeded. She was very unresponsive when we walked round except when we were shown a bedroom. She immediately said with great emphasis, 'I don't go in a bed.' In one of the day rooms they gave us tea. She had two sips and did manage some smiles for the other elderly residents. But when I got her home I had to manhandle her out of the car myself as no one was around to help. The trip was exhausting for both of us.

The home helps who were to come for the bedtime or morning shift once a week both made contact beforehand and witnessed the procedure. In each case I said I wouldn't go out when they were on duty but would be at the end of the phone in my house if they needed help. Neither of them did when the time came. As at South Park Mother put on her best behaviour for them.

The first Sunday at Dene Park was less successful. In fact she had only three Sundays there before we gave up. The authorities said her moaning emptied the day room and though it was up to me whether we continued I felt it was hardly fair on the other residents to have to put up with that.

In any event new family developments were bringing matters rapidly to a head. Two weddings were to take place in the summer, Mark's first and then Katherine's a month later and Claire, to everyone's delight, was expecting her first child in early September. There was no way I could share in these three joyful events unless Mother was being cared for full-time, even if it was only for short spells.

I made enquiries about respite care both at Dene Park and South Park. Dene Park could have had her for a week or a fortnight as required, but as residents were discouraged from using their bedrooms during the day and she had been so disruptive in the public room I didn't feel it would be right to send her there. South Park, on the other hand, was ideal but there were only two rooms left, a single and a shared. Mrs Watson had told me already that if I wanted the single room for Mother permanently she would be happy to have her. I had said I wasn't ready for that and indeed I knew that unless Mother's bungalow was sold and the money invested, we couldn't afford to do it. I had never thought to ask Mother to give me power of attorney over her affairs when she was still in her right mind, and it was too late to do it now when she couldn't sign her name to anything. I did approach our solicitor to set in train the procedure of applying for Court of Protection which was the only alternative remaining. But all that still seemed a long way off.

However, two nights when Mother actually bit me and hit me during the bedtime routine made me receptive to the Sister's urgency when she called and said, 'Don't leave it too long or your mother will be too bad to go to South Park.' I said, 'But I'll have to put the bungalow up for sale and then find out if Mrs Watson still has the single room available.' She said with great emphasis, 'Well, do it today.'

In a state of some trepidation and a feeling that things were moving beyond my control I rang round a few estate agents and picked the one I thought offered the best terms; they said they would send a valuer that afternoon. Luckily a friend was coming to see Mother so I asked her to sit with Mother in our house while the man went round her bungalow. Even though Mother would not have guessed his purpose I knew a strange man's presence would be disturbing. But I felt very guilty and deceptive till after he had gone and Mother was safely back.

Later I rang Mrs Watson and she said she was so sorry but someone else had an option on the only remaining single room and would be letting her know definitely after the weekend. I arranged to ring her on the Monday evening but I felt sure this must be the end of the matter.

When Alan came home I told him of the flurry of activity and we talked it all over earnestly. We tried to calculate what we could afford out of our own savings if the bungalow sale dragged on and whether we should try other Homes. But we prayed about it and I felt that when it was the right time for it to happen the Lord would open the door clearly and show us the way ahead.

On the Saturday it had been arranged for one of the home helps to be there to get Mother up and stay with her till the afternoon. It was a mild, breezy late February day and

Alan and I took the car and a picnic, drove into the country and climbed a high crag. It was a most strange and wonderful day. We just dwelt in the present moment, the freshness of the air, the scent of the moors, the feeling of the earth stirring with spring beneath our feet.

On the Monday evening I phoned Mrs Watson and she said the people were not taking up the option on the room and Mother could have it. My heart leapt, but I had to explain about the bungalow. I said we'd be happy to take up her offer at an unspecified date when it was sold. I thought she could let the room meanwhile for respite care which is always much in demand. We left it at that and I felt that the Lord had opened the door a little. Only time would show when and if the big change would happen.

The next morning Mrs Watson rang back and said she had been discussing it with her husband. She said, 'Would you like to bring your mother at once and we'll waive payment until you've got the finance from the bungalow sale?'

Suddenly the door was flung wide. This must be the answer. My head was in a whirl but I managed to say yes, with heartfelt thanks, and we agreed on 27th February, only one week away.

My feelings were very mixed. For whose sake was this happening? Mine or Mother's? Her eating had been so bad at home that it could only improve at South Park, and this might actually arrest what had been a rapid decline since the beginning of the year. At the same time I felt as if I was saying to God, 'Thanks for your help, but I'm throwing in the towel now.'

In fact the moment had come so suddenly and there was so much to see to that my mind could hardly encompass what was about to happen.

18
Mother goes into a Home

When we told the family and they realised how quickly Grandma and the contents of the bungalow would be gone, Katherine put all our thoughts into words: 'It's like wiping her off the map!' Of course, they all agreed it was the right decision but they had visited her there so happily for so long that it was hard to adjust to so swift a change.

It was an astonishing week. If I needed a sign that this was meant to happen I was given it at once. The doctor told me that her in-laws wanted to live in Hexham to be near them and would love to look at the bungalow. A friend from the Art Club said that it was just what *her* in-laws were looking for. Both families came to see it and for one of the visits I couldn't arrange for Mother to be elsewhere. She was quite smiley toward them and they wisely behaved just like friendly visitors but I couldn't tell if she guessed. Nothing was said. The same day the doctor's family offered the asking price and I accepted it. What had seemed a huge hurdle was over before I had drawn breath. Again the hand of God seemed to be hastening the move.

Everything had to be done now through the Court of Protection and this delayed the date of completion considerably so that it wasn't till August that we actually banked the money, but the Watsons never hassled us. Truly God was good to us in opening the way so plainly for what can be a long drawn-out, agonising, guilt-ridden decision for the carers in other cases like Mother's.

Katherine had had a very good idea before all this happened. Since Mother responded so well to babies she suggested I get her a doll to cuddle. I bought one of those squashy rubbery ones with integral dress, machine washable. She responded to it quite well but told one of the home helps, 'I don't think we ought to keep her.' Evidently she thought it was real! However, she was getting used to it before she went to South Park. I would sit it in front of her and make it clap its hands and once, actually smiling, she produced the longest sentence she had said for some time: 'I see no reason for you sitting there.' So the baby doll was to be a vital item in her luggage.

I spent some time that week marking her clothes just as if I was starting a child at boarding school. On the day before she was to go she suddenly said out of the blue, 'I don't want to go to that place.' I was really taken aback. Had she understood about South Park and been thinking about it? Of course, I had mentioned it several times – how happy she was going to be with her friends there and she would never have to be alone again night or day, and I would visit her every day, but she had never made the slightest response, just the 'Oh oh's and Lord, have mercy' which were now a perpetual refrain. Of course, she might just have been referring to the toilet which she was overdue to go to and which loomed larger in the scale of the miseries of her life than anything else. It was impossible to be sure.

That evening I couldn't believe it was the last time I would be putting her to bed. She was just as agitated as usual over the process but I sang to her to calm her down the hymn, 'How sweet the name of Jesus sounds'. This seemed to soothe her and I wondered why I hadn't sung to her more often. I could hardly get through the prayers I always said with her once she was in bed, I was so full of inward tears. She seemed so small and frail and I wondered how much longer she had to endure on this earth and whether I needed to make any change at all because the time might be so short.

Next day I took her to the Home and left her there, a shrunken, wizened figure with pinched, frightened face, crouched in a large armchair. Although everything had fallen into place so easily and seemed to point to this being the right thing for us both I still felt terribly guilty, strange and empty as I drove away.

The change for me was enormous. But for her too it was more than I had dared to hope. On 29th February I phoned before my visit and the diary records:

> I was told, 'She's eating like a horse. It took her only fifteen minutes to demolish her breakfast.' One of the girls had said to her, 'Did you enjoy your meal, then?' She replied, 'Yes, but not as much as yesterday's.' This is amazing on all counts, especially memory! She had porridge yesterday and cereal today, and bread and marmalade both days. I can't believe it! She has also been visited in her room by all her upstairs neighbours and has even consented to be taken downstairs to see the new budgie in its cage in the sitting-room.

Two things, I think, contributed to Mother's improved eating. One was the fact that she had been brought up very frugally and her teenage years were during the First World War. Even when she was grown-up and married it was a great treat for her to stay at a hotel, and on the rare occasions when she and my father did so she wouldn't have dreamt of leaving anything on her plate at mealtimes. The other factor, which affected her eating when I was looking after her, was her unselfishness as a mother. My sister and I were teenagers in the Second World War and during all the years of rationing Mother always put herself last. Somehow she sent us out to school with cooked breakfasts every day and made us substantial lunches at home too. She herself seemed to subsist on her home-made bread and dripping, the diet of her childhood.

I believe that subconsciously these two attitudes were behind the remarkable improvement in her eating when she went to South Park. She felt she was allowed to indulge herself, indeed she had an obligation to do so because someone – perhaps herself – was paying good money for it all and strangers were taking the trouble to serve it to her with great kindness. I don't think she had more appetite because by this time she didn't seem to connect hunger and thirst signals with the mechanics of eating and drinking. I just think deep-seated instincts were at work.

Over the first week of her stay we made gradual improvements in her room. The chair they'd provided was a swively one and I sensed she felt insecure in it so I brought one from home with wooden arms that she could grip. I also brought a little table and some of her pictures and a few more dresses. Claire and Katherine made separate visits with me early in her stay and she greeted each with a big smile of welcome. She wasn't talkative but she seemed content and the moaning of 'Oh oh's' had stopped. She must have felt stronger from being better nourished and they were delighted to see such an improvement in her.

One day I found her playing with the baby doll. She said it was sweet and stood it on its head and began chewing its foot. I said in a funny voice, 'Stop eating my foot' and

'I don't like standing on my head.' Mother laughed, looking from me to the doll to see where the voice was coming from, but went on biting its foot.

Of course, the dementia had not faded and though she produced occasional bursts of speech there was no doubt that the ability to talk was gradually leaving her altogether. As the weeks passed she became more apathetic and sometimes I doubted whether I ought to be stirring up her emotions when I said prayers with her and read the Bible. Often it made her cry, yet not to give her spiritual nourishment, to leave her in a glazed torpor, seemed very wrong. She did receive Communion with a group of residents in the Home and if I was visiting at the time I was always invited to participate. In general Mother seemed to take her cue from the rest and was quiet and sometimes responsive. She didn't weep in front of other people at that stage.

On 7th April 1988 I wrote:

> She was saying 'Eh, oh' over and over as I came into her room. I hoped it wasn't the start of moaning again so I said brightly, 'You're saying A and O, Alpha and Omega, the beginning and the end. You used to know the whole of the Greek alphabet – your brother John taught it to you as a child.' So I started to say, 'Alpha, Beta, Gamma – ' and she said, 'Delta' at once! Strange how the things learnt by heart in youth can be dredged up even in her poor old brain!

Thinking about her own family I remembered that I had never told her in so many words that her one remaining sister, Aunty Flo, had died at the age of ninety-seven. From then on I introduced her name in prayer among the dear ones the Lord would bring with him when he comes but Mother never commented on it.

I got no reaction either when I talked to her about my family, telling her about Mark and Katherine's weddings to come in the summer and Claire's baby on the way. Once I asked, 'Can you take that in?' She said, 'I shan't even try,' which at least showed she had understood my question.

Alan and I had a ten-day camping holiday in the highlands at the end of May, visiting places my parents and Janet and I had been to when I was three, places which Mother had always spoken of with great delight. On my first visit after our return I said, 'We've been camping.' She said in a quite matter-of-fact voice, 'Well, you do things of that sort.' So I tried to interest her in the wildlife we'd seen but she just gazed around, not listening. Then I said, 'Do Loch an Eileen and Tulloch Grubh mean anything to you?' and she said, 'Oh, yes,' with a little smile. Again, echoes of the far past could still trigger a response.

It was heartening to know that she hadn't been fretting in my absence but all of us who visited her now, friends and family, got the impression that she was no longer aware of time at all. Speech was almost gone and in its place the low moaning was returning. The initial effort of the first six months at South Park had worn itself out and the final phase of dementia was closing in.

19
The End of the Road

Mother lingered in deep dementia till seven weeks past her ninetieth birthday, so she was actually in the Home for one year and ten months, wonderfully loved and cared for by the Watsons and all the staff.

She was shown the photographs of Katherine's and Mark's weddings. She held in her arms little Alice, Claire's beautiful baby, and we photographed them together, but her love of children had given way to mere bewilderment. On warm days she sat out in the grounds or I took her out in a wheelchair provided by the Home, but even the sunshine she had always enjoyed so much produced hardly any reaction.

There were still rare glimpses, though, of the person she had once been. Vi, one of the most sensitive of all the caring staff, told me one day how she had been bringing in Mother's tea tray and her apron bow had caught on the door handle. She jerked back and nearly spilt the tray. Mother, looking round from her chair, had reached out her arms to her with a yearning, anxious look and brought out a gasping, 'Oh, darling – !' Vi had laid down the tray and soothed away her concern with, 'It's all right. I'm all right, don't worry.' But she said it was one of the many tiny ways in which they could see what a lovely character my mother truly was.

Still, during those many frustrating visits, when I could see only the cloud of misery which seemed to surround her, I prayed often for some response, for smiles, for her just to be at peace. I even wondered if she had rejected me because I had put her there and caused her unhappiness.

I don't know when exactly it was, as I had ceased to write the journal, but it must have been sometime in the summer of 1989, that I had an unforgettable spiritual experience as a result of one of these times of prayer. Mother was sitting in her chair, rocking herself as if in deep distress, when I went in. I knelt down beside her and my first feelings were those of anger, anger with her for not being a placid sufferer as some of them were in the Home, perpetually smiling and benign, and anger with God for allowing her to go on living like this. I didn't pray coherently. Rather it seemed to me that I wrestled with God as Jacob did, in a spiritual battle. But all at once my tears stopped flowing and a deep peace descended. I felt the most amazing sense of God's love surrounding me and Mother. I kissed and hugged her and though she continued to sit apathetically I went out from there as if walking in heaven. The few people I saw on my way home I loved and embraced in my heart as they passed. I was singing inside as I prepared Alan's evening meal and the joy clung to me like stardust well into the next day. I can recall it perfectly whenever I think of it.

I will never again agonise over the mystery of suffering. Pain and illness and death are not good things, they are part of the evil which, like sin, is still rampant in the world, but if we allow God to work they can be the focus of the most amazing love. Why Mother had to go through that trial was not for me to know. Perhaps it was inevitable that the active, busy soul she was could not endure the loss of ability to be perpetually doing. Maybe her spirit, deep inside, was undergoing a needful testing and purifying, a baptism of fire. Only God knows. What I realised through that wonderful experience and over the whole time of her decline was that her presence amongst us was our call to love, a selfless love, a love without boundaries.

She finally slipped away on the last day of 1989 after the Rector had conducted a short service for the dying. I tried to make her funeral a time of joy rather than sorrow, because almost as soon as she was dead I felt suddenly close to the Mother I had always known from babyhood, the bright, eager, unselfish soul remembered by all her family. I knew that the sad veil of senility had been shed for ever and she was at peace.

But of all the cards and letters that I received, nearly all evoking happy memories of her in her younger days, the one that moved me most was from the staff of South Park. They said how much they had all loved her and how they would miss her. What had they seen, I thought, apart from those last twenty-two months of her sad decline? And yet, somehow, as they had ministered to her in kindness, she in turn had been ministering to them. She had brought out the best in them all, that wonderful quality of LOVE, which I understood so much more deeply after this long-drawn out and often painful trial.

The day will come when she and I will laugh together again and I will tell her, 'You thought you were condemned to a non-existence, a hard road at the end, for one so creatively active, but even there you were achieving something wonderful, perhaps more than you could ever imagine.'

Her gravestone bears the simple legend, 'Awaiting a joyful resurrection'. May that glorious day of the Lord come soon to bless the whole sad world.

The Alzheimer's Society is the leading care and research charity for people with all forms of dementia, their families and carers. It is dependent on donations for its work. If you would like to find out more or make a donation please ring 020 7306 0821.

The Alzheimer's Helpline, available from Monday-Friday, is 0845 300 0336.